Craft of Woodturning

John Sainsbury

Illustrations
A. G. Walker

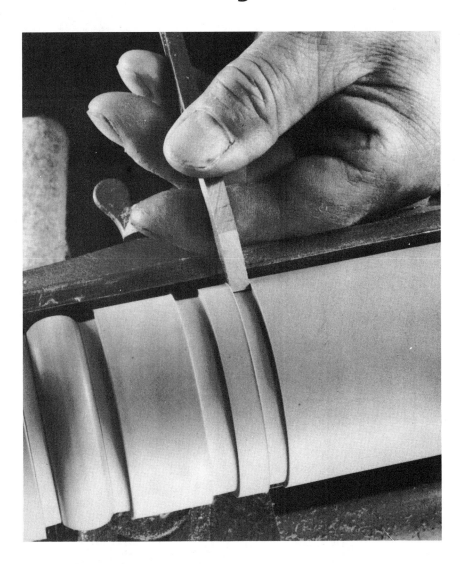

 Sterling Publishing Co., Inc. New York

Distributed in the U.K. by Blandford Press

Library of Congress Cataloging in Publication Data

Sainsbury, John A.
  The craft of woodturning.

  Includes index.
  1. Turning. I. Title.
TT202.S24 1984   684′.083   83-24118
ISBN 0-8069-5518-X
ISBN 0-8069-7828-7 (pbk.)

Revised edition copyright © 1984 John Sainsbury
Published by Sterling Publishing Co., Inc.
Two Park Avenue, New York, N.Y. 10016
First edition published in England © 1980 McGraw-Hill Book
Company (UK) Limited, Maidenhead, Berkshire, England
Distributed in Australia by Oak Tree Press Co., Ltd.
P.O. Box K514 Haymarket, Sydney 2000, N.S.W.
Distributed in the United Kingdom by Blandford Press
Link House, West Street, Poole, Dorset BH15, 1LL, England
Distributed in Canada by Oak Tree Press Ltd.
℅ Canadian Manda Group, P.O. Box 920, Station U
Toronto, Ontario, Canada M8Z 5P9
Manufactured in the United States of America

Contents

Preface

My interest in woodturning goes back many years, to the time I was engaged in teaching school. Little information was available in those days and proficiency came with patient experiment. The children became both my pupils and my teachers; at the same time the need to present them with craft perfection necessitated the pursuit of safe methods. The inadequacies of lathe equipment presented the need to design ancillary gear to widen the scope of the work.

Later, my association with Record Ridgway Tools Ltd. as Educational and Technical Adviser gave me the opportunity to study the cutting tools and to some extent influence their design. Lectures and demonstrations all over the world, to a wide range of audiences, including teachers, gave me the chance to influence the woodturner in the search for sound techniques. This is a continuing process, but nowadays people come from many parts to my Craft Studio in Devon. This book has therefore been written to record much of this experience. The camera has been used to enable the reader to see the tools through the eye of the turner. These, and the many line drawings, thanks to the skill of Tony Walker, serve to clarify the text.

The craft of woodturning is a fascinating one, and once the skill has been acquired, your enjoyment of it can be infinite. The argument about cutting and scraping will continue for many years, but the mastery of the cutting tools and the ultimate success in seeing the ribboned shavings flying should be the aim of all aspiring woodturners. I'd like to think that this book will make a worthwhile contribution to them.

JOHN SAINSBURY

Acknowledgements

For permission to use illustrations and other details of their products, the author wishes to express his thanks to

Acre (Willington) Ltd, Willington, Derbyshire
Black & Decker Tools Ltd, Maidenhead, Berkshire
Coronet Tool Co. Ltd, Alfreton Road, Derby
Craft Supplies, The Mill, Millersdale, Buxton, Derbyshire
Denford Machine Tools Ltd, Brighouse, Yorkshire
E.M.E. Ltd, BEC House, Victoria Road, London
Myford Engineering Co. Ltd, Beeston, Nottinghamshire
Peter Child, The Old Hyde, Great Yeldham, Halstead, Essex
Rockwell International, Pittsburgh, Pa., USA
Tyme Machines (Bristol) Ltd., Kingswood, Bristol
T. S. Harrison & Son Ltd, Union Works, Heckmondwike,
    Yorkshire
Wolf Electric Tools Ltd, Hanger Lane, London

The author seeks also to thank the Chief Executive and Directors of Record Ridgway Tools Ltd, Sheffield, for their encouragement and permission to use half tones and line drawings of tools of their manufacture.

His special appreciation must also go to

Tony Walker for many line drawings
Elspeth Flowerday for endless patience in typing the manuscript
Peter Baylis for his skilful reading, correction and guidance
Many friends, colleagues and teacher-pupils who have helped in various ways to bring this book to completion.

1 The Lathe and its Equipment

Types of lathe

There are many excellent lathes available throughout the world. They can be divided roughly into three groups. First, those built with teaching in mind, which tend to be very highly safety-proofed and sturdy, to give hard wear over a long period. Secondly, those often built as multipurpose machines for the home user, incorporating circular saw, bandsaw, sanding table, and other features. These are intended for the home craftsman, but one or two are sturdy enough to be used on limited production work. In this group will also be found a small lathe which uses an electric drill as its power unit. Thirdly, industrial machines, either automatic or manual, the former giving high output and requiring no hand skill.

All of these lathes have the same basic features, but additional facilities vary from one lathe design to another and may depend to a certain extent on the cost of the lathe itself. Many woodturning lathes of the past seem to have been made by the engineer without regard for the user, although it would have been much more sensible for the designer to have sought the advice and drawn upon the experience of the craftsman/teacher/user. Certainly, terms of reference should include details of holding devices which will accommodate many different sizes of timber and the various types of job which can be done. Alteration of speeds and adjustment of belts is often difficult and even hazardous to the hands. Tool rests need especial care in their design and manufacture, and particular attention needs to be paid to their length and shape. Many lathe components are over-built, so far as weight is concerned, which indicates some woolly thinking on the part of the manufacturer and little real knowledge of the function of each of the component parts. A handbrake would be a useful addition, while levers should be easy of access and free from obstruction to avoid injury to the hands.

Perhaps the most significant advance in lathe design in recent years is found in the Acre Varispeed. Sturdily built, this lathe is the first in the UK with an infinitely variable speed mechanism which eliminates belt changing in the traditional way. Instant speed adjustment with the machine running fulfils a long-felt need and eliminates the necessity for doors, microswitches, catches, etc. It saves time and avoids difficult movement of belts and trapping of the fingers.

This machine also incorporates a headstock spindle locking lever which provides a positive hold when removing faceplates and also serves to break the electrical circuit to avoid accidental running of the lathe with the headstock locked. This lathe has the usual attachments and is beautifully finished in a hammered stove enamel.

Fig. 1.1
Acre Varispeed lathe

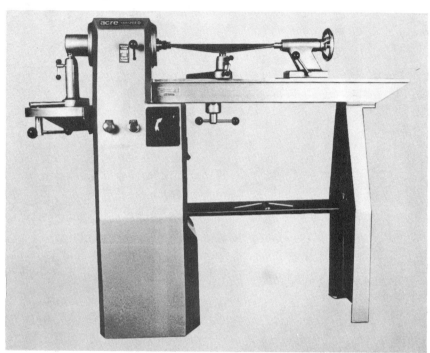

There is also a short-bed version, which is particularly useful where space is limited and where the user may not be turning long lengths between centres.

Fig. 1.2
Acre Varispeed short-bed lathe

The Harrison Graduate is a heavily built lathe with cast iron pedestals and a solid machined bed. It is available in normal-bed or long-bed length, or short-bed length with 14 in. (350 mm) between centres, or as a simple bowl-turning head.

Fig. 1.3
Harrison Graduate lathe

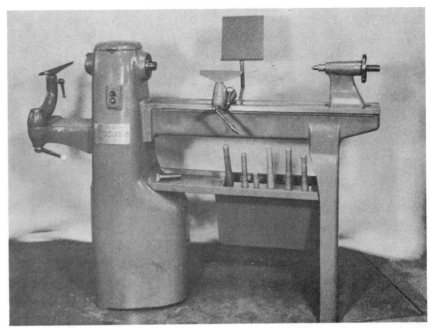

Fig. 1.4
Harrison short-bed graduate lathe

Fig. 1.5
Harrison bowl-turning head

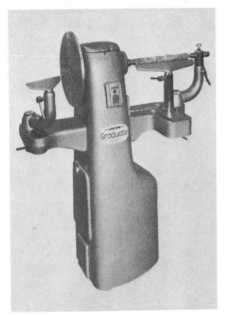

The Denford Viceroy is in the traditional style with locking device for the headstock spindle. Both the Harrison and the Denford machines have a motor-lifting lever to make for easier belt changing.

One of the most popular machines throughout the world is the Myford ML8, which incorporates all the facilities for woodturning with an extremely fine range of accessories. This is an ideal machine for the home user.

Fig. 1.7
Myford ML8 lathe

Fig. 1.6
Denford Viceroy lathe

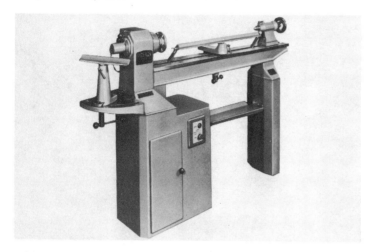

Fig. 1.8
Coronet Major lathe

Fig. 1.9
Tyme Avon lathe

Coronet have a number of variations in their woodturning range, including the Major and the Minor.

An ideal lathe for the homeworker is the Tyme Avon. Here, the need for right- and left-hand faceplates and other attachments is eliminated, since the headstock unit can be turned from the inside position to the outboard position for large work.

A simpler lathe is the Elf, manufactured by Coronet, which is ideal for the home craftsman, and is also useful for schools.

The Rockwell Beaver Model 3400 is a gap-bed lathe giving a 15 in. (380 mm) swing in the gap and 11 in. (275 mm) in the bed. It is fitted with lifetime lubricated bearings and has four speeds.

The ELU DB180 lathe is of die-cast construction with several innovative ideas.

Fig. 1.10
Coronet Elf lathe

Fig. 1.11
The ELU DB180 lathe features a 1500-watt motor, three speeds and live ball-bearing tail centre. Length between centres allows pieces up to 380 mm in diameter to be turned.

5

Attachments

A number of lathe attachments for the electric drill are available, one of the most popular being the Black & Decker attachment. Work can be carried out between centre and faceplate, with limitation on size being the only drawback. The need for speed control arises with this type of machine and the user would be well advised to build a small control box.

Fig. 1.12
Black & Decker lathe attachment for the electric drill

Future design

There are a number of designs for home-made lathes, which are simple enough to be within the capabilities of the average home craftsman or school craft department.

The perfect tool has not yet been designed, neither has the perfect lathe for wood-turning—but we live in hope.

The lathe and its parts

The woodturning lathe is of very simple construction when compared with its metalworking counterpart.

The timber to be turned needs to be securely mounted at both ends if spindle work is envisaged, or it must be fixed in some way if blocks are to be used. At the same time, provision must be made to turn the material at a predetermined speed. This is accomplished by a spindle mounted in bearings in a headstock.

Fig. 1.13
Two-prong centre

The spindle or mandrel is usually threaded at both ends to receive various components and bored to receive a Morse tapered driving fork. Such spindles require both right- and left-hand threaded components.

At the other end is a centre which does not rotate (usually called dead centre) but supports the spindle timber. This is mounted in the tailstock (usually bored to a Morse taper) which has an adjustable sleeve to enable the centre to be wound into the timber. The sleeve is firmly held by the thumbscrew or lever.

Fig. 1.14
Cup centre

The headstock is fixed to a bed at the left-hand end, while the tail-stock can be moved freely to any position along it and locked firmly in place by a lever action.

Fitted at the left-hand end or outboard of the headstock is a bowl unit to facilitate the turning of larger work than can be accommodated within the height-of-centres capacity between centres. Large faceplates are supplied with left-hand threads, unless the headstock can be swivelled.

Fig. 1.15
Outboard unit for turning larger work

There are three types of tailstock centre—solid, cup and rotating. Each type has its own particular features. The use of the cup centre ensures positive engagement of the long-hole boring attachment when boring holes in table and standard lamps. The impression made in the timber by the cup ring exactly locates the attachment.

The solid centre permits use of tools almost up the centre of the timber, a highly desirable facility in some work.

Fig. 1.16
Tailstock centre (solid)

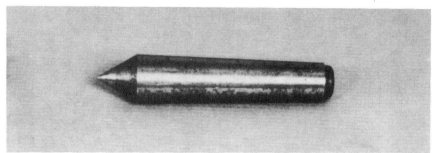

Fig. 1.17
Tailstock centre (cup)

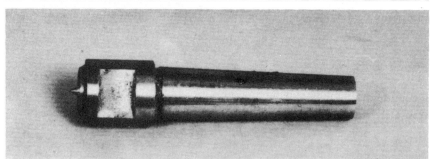

Fig. 1.18
Tailstock centre (running)

The rotating centre will not burn the timber because it rotates with it; lubricating grease or oil is therefore unnecessary.

The headstock mandrel Morse taper accommodates a two-prong or a four-prong centre.

A useful four-prong centre, which incorporates a plug centre, is used when lamp standard timber has been bored half-way and then reversed to complete the boring. The plug centre fits the hole and if a mortise is required at this end to receive the other half of a tall standard lamp,

Fig. 1.19
Headstock mandrel Morse taper (two-prong centre)

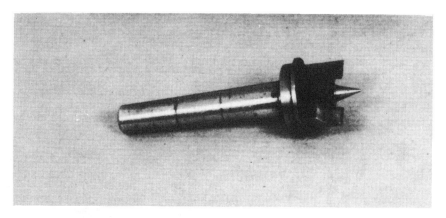

Fig. 1.20
Headstock mandrel Morse taper (four-prong centre)

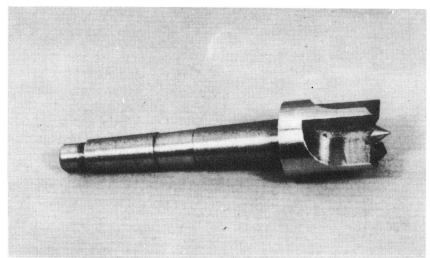

then by using the tailstock centre to push the wood hard against the plug centre, the prongs act as cutters in the same way as a counterbore.

The headstock screw will accommodate various sizes of faceplate, on to which timber can be fixed with countersunk screws from the back.

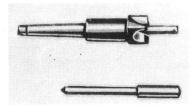

Fig. 1.21
Coronet counterboring tool

Fig. 1.22
Headstock with faceplates at left- and right-hand ends

Fig. 1.23
3-in. faceplate

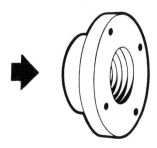

Fig. 1.24
Faceplate

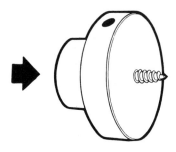

The screw-flange chuck has a single screw on to which timber can be mounted. Often, these chucks have an additional screw hole in the flange through which a countersunk screw can be fitted to act as an extra hold for the wood.

The collar chuck (sometimes called an egg-cup chuck, a term which erroneously indicates its use solely in the making of egg-cups) has many applications. Timber has to be prepared between centres to fit this chuck. The collar chuck is described in more detail later (see page 17).

Fig. 1.25
Screw-flange chuck

Fig. 1.26
Collar (egg-cup) chuck

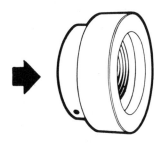

Fig. 1.27
Collar (egg-cup) chuck

Fig. 1.28
Planing timber between centres to fit collar chuck

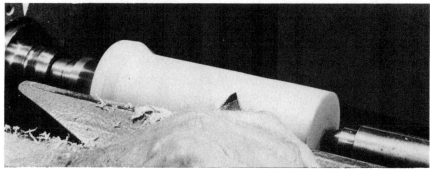

Fig. 1.29
Timber planed to shape and size

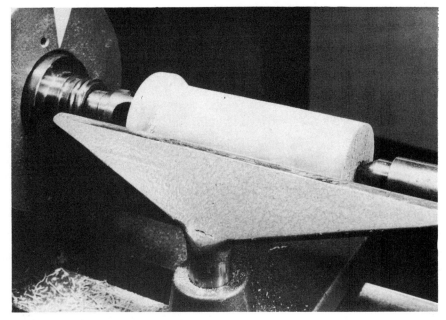

Fig. 1.30
Preparation of timber for the collar chuck

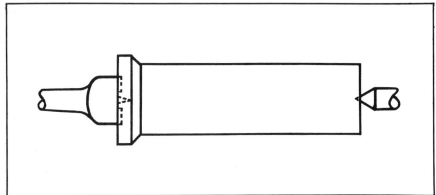

Fig. 1.31
Preparation of timber for the collar chuck

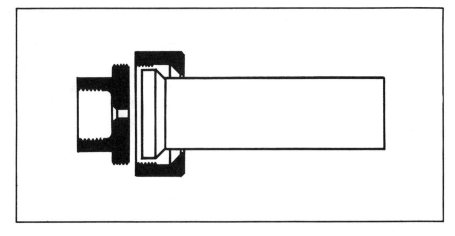

A chuck which surpasses all others in its universality is the six-in-one combination chuck manufactured by Hattersley & Davidson in England. The chuck not only includes most of the features of others previously mentioned, but also incorporates an expanding collet which enables timber to be held in a recess cut in the base of the turning. This chuck and its various uses are described in detail later (see page 17).

A normal collet chuck is also made by the same company. This chuck permits the holding of spindle wood up to 1 in. (25 mm) in diameter or timber prepared between centres with a spigot at one end. Three sizes of collet are provided, permitting capacities of ½, ¾ and 1 in. (13, 19 and 25 mm).

Fig. 1.32
Precision combination chuck with expanding collet

Fig. 1.33
Precision combination chuck, fitted with a spigot

A variation of the collar chuck is the Myford three-in-one type, which not only provides the collar-chuck facility but also has an insert disc to convert to a screw chuck; with both collar and disc removed it becomes a faceplate.

Fig. 1.34
Myford three-in-one chuck

Fig. 1.35
Tyme screw chuck set

Another useful type is the Child chuck, which was designed by Roy Child, the son of Peter Child the well-known woodturner. This chuck is a faceplate, screw chuck and collar chuck combined, but the collar chuck enables timber to be held by a unique split collar device or a coil. This permits the holding of timber of any diameter within the capacity

13

Fig. 1.36
Child chuck

of the lathe centre height. Preparation of the timber, between centres, is necessary and accurate measurement of groove size and diameter is essential.

Another attachment for the headstock is the cup chuck. It is described more fully later (see page 21).

Fig. 1.37
Tyme cup chuck set

Tool rests come in various lengths, but no manufacturer makes a really short one.

For bowl scraping, a curved rest is useful, enabling close cutting inside the work.

To facilitate the boring of holes, a drill chuck fitted with a Morse taper arbor to suit the lathe is essential.

Some lathe heads can be swivelled, thus excluding the need for left- and right-hand faceplates (Coronet and Tyme Avon).

Fig. 1.38
Tool rests

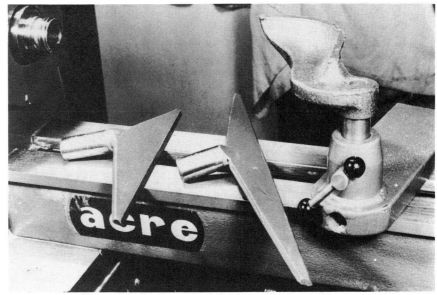

Fig. 1.39
Curved rest for bowl scraping

Fig. 1.40
Tailstock—drill chuck

To support the wood for long-hole boring and, at the same time, to provide an aperture through which an auger can be passed, most lathe manufacturers produce long-hole boring attachments. One design fits on the tailstock sleeve nose, while another replaces the tool rest.

Power for the lathe is usually provided by an electric motor. A ¾ h.p. motor will be sufficient for most lathes, but those of extremely heavy construction may require a 1 h.p. single-phase 240 V or three-phase 400V, or 110 V for the American market.

The motor is usually fitted with a three- or four-step pulley which is matched by one on the headstock mandrel, but reversed in order to give a choice of speeds. Lathes like the Varispeed are an exception to this arrangement, whereas the Wessex has six speeds by a simple re-arrangement of the pulleys.

Fig. 1.41
Long-hole boring attachment—tailstock type

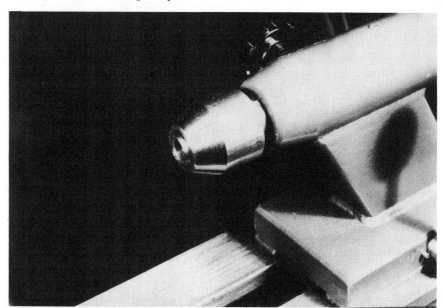

Fig. 1.42
Long-hole boring attachment—long standard lamp shell auger

Additional holding equipment available for most lathes

Faceplates

These plates are available in many sizes, both left and right hand, and are designed to enable blocks of wood to be held for turning. For the average small lathe, plates of 3 in. and 4 in. (76 and 100 mm) will be sufficient to hold most work. Larger faceplates often up to the 'swing' size of the lathe are available, both left and right hand.

Screw chuck

The screw chuck screws on to the headstock mandrel. It is fitted with a stout screw placed centrally in the plate and held in place by a grub screw. Small pieces of wood can safely be held in place by the screw while they are turning. Where very thin timber is to be turned, pieces of ⅛ in. (3 mm) hardboard on the face of the chuck may be used to reduce the length of screw and prevent it breaking through. These discs of hardboard can also serve to support the larger discs of wood in the peripheral area during turning. A hole must be bored in the disc to clear the screw. Any swelling around the hole of either the disc or the wood will prevent the wood seating properly. Tight and accurate seating is essential to ensure perfect cutting.

When turning smaller pieces, the hardboard serves to protect the tools and faceplate against accident. The hardboard will also help to support small picture frames and rings when parting off timber up to 8 in. (203 mm) × 1 in. (25 mm) for plate and mirror frame work, or small bowl blocks up to 3½ in. (89 mm) diameter by 2½–3 in. (63–76 mm) length maximum sizes of timber.

Collar chuck or ring chuck

A workpiece is prepared with a small flange at one end. The body of the chuck screws on to the headstock and the wood is passed through the ring. By screwing up the ring on to the chuck body, the flange is held inside, securely holding the work. Most chucks will hold timber up to 2 in. (50 mm) in diameter.

Expanding collet chuck

Probably the greatest advance in woodturning chucks is the Hattersley & Davidson, six-in-one Universal chuck. This has all the features of the earlier mentioned Child chuck, except for the coil, but it incorporates a unique feature—an expanding collet.

The outside of the article is turned first, the timber being held on a faceplate or, alternatively, by a special ring designed by the same company. A shallow recess is cut in the base with a dovetailed lip. The four-section dovetail collet fits into the recess and, by screwing down on the chuck collar, the bowl can be held securely for final turning. A smaller and a larger collet are also available as optional extras.

The ring holding the timber not only has a dovetailed recess cut in it to accommodate the expanding collet but also has three countersunk screw holes which enable it to be substituted for the faceplate for first turning. The use of faceplates is therefore eliminated and expense to the turner is reduced.

Fig. 1.43
Six-in-one Universal chuck

Fig. 1.44
Six-in-one chuck ring

The expanding collet chuck can serve as a screw chuck

Plane the work flat and mark the centre. Drill a pilot hole for the screw. Assemble the chuck on the lathe and screw the wood on to the chuck. Hardboard washers may be found useful to facilitate access to the back of the work. The screw (No. 14) can be replaced or adjusted to protrude the desired amount by using the Allen key. Exercise care when screwing into end-grain work.

Fig. 1.45
Six-in-one as a screw chuck

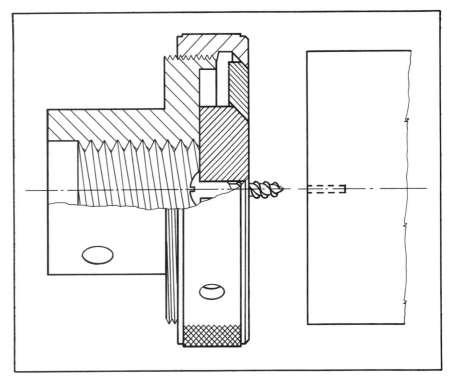

The expanding collet chuck can serve as a threaded cup chuck (internal screw chuck)

Prepare the work between centres to provide a spigot, as shown. Using the tailstock to provide pressure and to centralize the work, screw the spigot into the central hole in the chuck body as far as it will go. Do not remove and replace, as this weakens the grip. Do not use for side-grain work. Take care not to damage the outside thread of the cup chuck when turning or when removing from the lathe. A precaution to avoid damage is to screw on the collar from the rear.

Fig. 1.46
Six-in-one as a threaded cup chuck

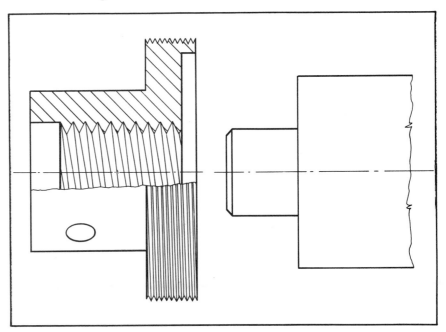

The expanding collet chuck can serve as a faceplate (use the body on its own)

Use with three screws as usual. For some jobs, a plywood or hard-board washer to fill the recess is useful.

The expanding collet chuck can serve as a split ring chuck

Similar to the collar chuck, previously described, but not only can the collar itself be used to secure the timber but also a split ring inserted inside the collar can be used to secure any size of timber within the capacity of the lathe.

Fig. 1.47
Six-in-one chuck—using split collar to mount wood chuck

Mount the wood between centres and produce a square-end face and the groove as shown (the use of a sizing tool with ⅜ in. (9.5 mm) beading and parting tool simplifies this operation). Assemble the chuck on the lathe and grip the wood as shown. This is suitable for wood of between 1¾ in. (45 mm) and 2½ in. (63 mm). For material larger than 2½ in., prepare the wood between centres and turn an additional 1⁵⁄₁₆ in. (33 mm) or 2½ in. to allow for the ⅜ in. (9.5 mm) groove before assembling the split ring.

Coil chuck

A similar chuck to the six-in-one (expanding collet) type is the Child coil chuck. It has all the features except the expanding collet, but includes an additional and extremely clever device using a coiled spring to locate and hold the workpiece.

This is a front-entry type of collar chuck. The only capacity limit on this chuck is the maximum diameter of block which the swing of the lathe will permit.

Prepare the wood between centres to provide a flange as shown. Dimensions are critical. Assemble the chuck on the lathe with the spring held loosely inside. Pass the flange through the ring into the recess in the chuck body. Hold it there while screwing up the ring.

Fig. 1.48
Child coil chuck—timber prepared for holding using the coil spring

Tighten securely using the pin spanner. For large work in soft wood, re-tighten occasionally during the turning operation. To remove the wood, unscrew the ring until the flange is released.

Collet chuck

This chuck has been developed to grip timber up to a diameter of $1^1/_{16}$ in. (27 mm). It also allows the holding of timber where it is possible to produce a spigot which can be inserted and held securely in the collet.

Cup chuck

This screws on to the headstock and is recessed to receive timber which has already been turned to size. Ideal for small boxes and vases.

A home-made cup chuck can be made from a block of wood screwed to a faceplate.

Fig. 1.49
Collet chuck

Fig. 1.50
Metal tee-rest with timber insert

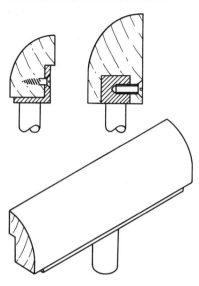

The tee-rest

The lathe manufacturer, probably of necessity, makes a solid metal rest which in use needs constant attention from the file and is cold to the hand. The woodturner often finds the lengths inadequate—the long one is often not long enough, or the short one is too short—and with very short work between centres, it is often impossible to get the standard rest close to the work.

The rule when using the rest is that it should at all times be placed as close to the work as possible. Its height will depend on the type of tool being used, but a general guide is: for work between centres the tee-rest should be fractionally above centre, while for bowl work it should be fractionally below centre.

However, when using the chisel for spindle turning between centres, the rest should be as high as possible so that the chisel cuts the work at a point slightly below top dead centre.

Long and strong gouges will need the rest lower than standard gouges to allow for the greater thickness of the tool.

In use, the rest should permit the tool to move smoothly along the length of the work without being impeded. The best type of rest is a wooden one made from long straight-grained hardwood, screwed either to a steel bar or a piece of angle iron. Any number of rests can be made up and the timber insert can be cut to any length as needed. This type of rest can be planed true with a steel jack plane either *in situ* or on the bench.

Fig. 1.51
Egg-cup template

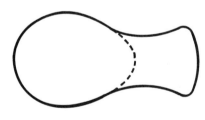

Fig. 1.52
Temco template

Use of templates

The use of templates is necessary, particularly where repetition work is to be carried out.

In many cases, a straight 'take-off' of a cardboard template from a drawing will suffice.

Articles such as egg-cups require a degree of accuracy both in shape and size, and in these cases it is advisable to cut templates from thin sheet aluminium.

Coat the edge of the template with waxed crayon. When held to the revolving work, the crayon rubs off on the high spots.

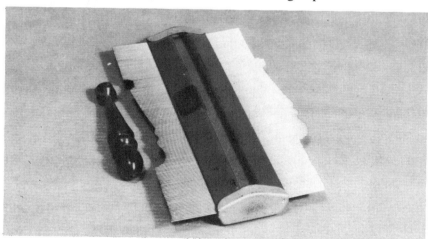

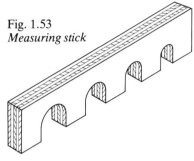

Fig. 1.53
Measuring stick

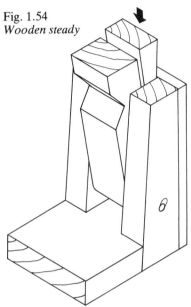

Fig. 1.54
Wooden steady

An extremely useful tool is the Temco template. It is infinitely adjustable and an exact copy can be taken from an existing piece of turned work.

When timber is being turned down to a number of fixed diameters, a measuring stick indicating the various diameters will be found useful.

Steadies

From time to time slender work will need to be turned. No matter how sharp or how correctly the tools are used, the thin timber will tend to move away from the tool. The resultant 'chatter' will not only offend the ear but the timber surface will spiral and give an unacceptable finish.

Many experienced woodturners support the work with the left hand, at the same time holding the chisel down on the work, but care has to be taken to support the wood lightly to avoid burning the hand. The position of the hand must be watched as it moves towards the driving fork, otherwise carelessness may result in serious injury.

A useful steady can be made from wood and attached to the rear of the lathe bed, but great care must be exercised in its use to avoid burning the work.

The author has for many years used a steady designed for the Myford lathe. This is simply a pair of rubber-tyred toy wheels mounted on a sprung arm. As the wood is turned down in front of the steady, the wheels automatically move forward to support the work.

Fig. 1.55
Steady for Myford ML8

Fig. 1.56
Meccano wheel steady in use on Myford ML8

2 Safety on the Lathe

General safety rules

Woodturning can be a wholly enjoyable craft, but in order that this shall be the experience of both schoolchildren and adults, strict attention must be paid to safety. Safety can be broadly divided and contained in four areas: (1) safety to the person, (2) safety in regard to the machine itself, (3) safety to both person and machine when the machine is running, and (4) safe materials.

The turner must be properly attired. He should wear an apron or dust coat. If he is wearing a tie, it is best either to remove it or clip it to another part of his clothing so that it cannot fall freely over the lathe. Shirt sleeves or sleeves of any kind should be rolled up and long hair tied back. Suitable goggles of the anti-misting type should be worn for protection of the eyes and these must be kept in perfect condition. Ladies should wear a net over the hair or use some other means of keeping the hair back.

The lathe should be bolted to the floor or set upon a suitable mat. Press button starters should be of the no-volt and overload-protection type on both single- and three-phase a.c. voltages. If access to the belt or belts is through doors or panels, then these must be fitted with micro-switches which break the circuit, enabling adjustments to be made without any danger of the motor being switched on. The switch should be so

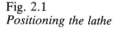
Fig. 2.1
Positioning the lathe

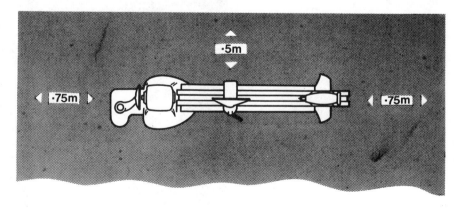

placed on the machine, with ease of access to the hand, that the operator can reach it without bending and without the necessity of looking for it. Securely fix all component parts of the lathe. It is essential for the tee-rest to be straight and true; that is, when fixed to the tool post slide it should be parallel with the lathe bed. The chisels of the driving fork must be sharp and the centre point and the tailstock dead centre should be in good condition. All moving parts should be lubricated to ensure ease of movement.

In a school or college workshop, site the lathe so that the teacher, no matter in what part of the room he may be standing, can see both the operator and the work. This may necessitate the angling of the lathe to the wall, and, if this is done, then sufficient space must be left on the left-hand end of the machine for the operator to work without being obstructed by the wall or other machinery. The lathe must have adequate daylight and artificial light. Where tubular lighting is in use, then this must be anti-stroboscopic. However, bearing in mind that this type of lighting is non-directional, it is advisable to fit each machine with a transformer to give 12 V d.c. lighting.

Before switching on the lathe, make sure that the work will rotate freely without being obstructed by the tee-rest. Be sure, too, that the correct speed is being used. This will, of course, relate to the size of the timber being turned and whether the work is spindle or faceplate. All tools must be correctly sharpened, particular attention being paid to sharpening on the ground bevel and, in the case of gouges, ensuring that they are shaped correctly. The rule of the lathe in cutting, and this is of course basic safety, is that the bevel of the tool should rub the wood (it should never cut when first placed on the tool rest). The tool will cut when the right hand is raised. This brings the centre of the chisel or gouge into direct contact with the wood. The tool also slopes in the direction of travel; thus, a slicing cut is taken. This, again, is an added safety precaution.

If scraping tools are used, these must be sharpened correctly and, unlike the cutting tools, they must rest firmly on the tee-rest and be trailed; that is, they slope downwards. In this way, they cut exactly like the cabinet maker's scraper on the bench. The tool must, of course, be correctly held, lightly but firmly with the left hand across the tool and well up to the cutting edge. This will result in the shavings being moved away from the user's face. Place the tool rest as close to the work as possible and at the correct height.

Fig. 2.2
In scraping—the tool trails

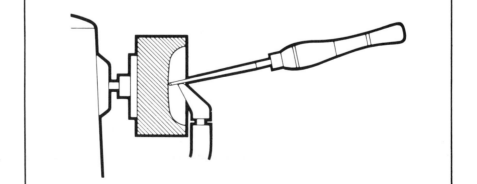

The correct height will depend upon the type of tool being used; for example, the thickness of a long and strong gouge will need the tee-rest to be placed slightly lower than if a standard gouge is being used. The general rule is that the tee-rest for spindle work should be slightly above centre, while for bowl work it should be slightly below centre. Never move the tee-rest with the lathe switched on.

A revolving centre is best in the tailstock, but if this accessory is not available a small spot of grease applied to the dead centre will reduce friction and prevent burning.

When glasspapering, the tee-rest must be completely removed. The glasspaper should be cut to a comfortable size and preferably backed with a pad to prevent the fingers being burned should the glasspaper be applied too firmly. The pad must be held in the right hand and the left hand used as a support. This brings both hands into use and will possibly prevent accidents by careless placement of the hand on the headstock. In spindle work the paper should be applied underneath, whereas in bowl work it should be placed inside the bowl in a 'clock position' of between half past and a quarter to.

Polish should be applied with the machine in the rest position, again using a small pad. Trailing cloths should be avoided. Burnishing of the polish should take place with the machine running and the pad applied in the same way as when glasspapering. The practice of burnishing with shavings is a sound one, so long as a ball of shavings is used and applied in the same way as the polishing cloth. Great care must be taken, in all three operations, to avoid excessive pressure since both wood and hands can be burned.

Careful selection of the timber for woodturning is essential (see page 62). Often, too little attention is paid to this point. One must at all times remember that the lathe is revolving at high speed and any material leaving it by accident could be lethal either to the user or to other people in the workshop. Never use timber with cracks or splits, loose knots or flaws, beetle holes or deep resin ducts. If reclaimed timber is being used, examine it very carefully for nails and other metallic objects. Scrutinize very carefully timber collected from the fields and hedgerows for wire, wire staples, nails, bolts or lead shot. If there is any doubt about any piece of timber, the golden rule is, no matter how attractive, do not use it. The use of built-up blocks is not to be encouraged.

Timber can be held on the lathe in various ways, but if blocks are to be held on the faceplate they must be screwed firmly to it with stout screws and the timber itself be flat to the faceplate to enable security to be obtained. If the screw-flange chuck is being used, a limit should be placed on the length of the timber, particularly if the screw is inserted in end grain. A large soft-leather washer inserted between the face of the chuck and the work will take up any irregularities in the work and any slight swelling around the hole. Wherever possible, bring up the tailstock to increase the support. If a collar chuck is in use, the collar must be screwed down by hand, and again it is essential for the left-hand end of the timber to be square and flat and coming into close abutment with the back plate of the collar chuck. If a wood chuck is being used to hold an article, the tee-rest must be brought tight up to the chuck and slightly above centre, so that if the article breaks loose it will revolve inside the wood chuck without it being possible for it to fly out of the chuck itself.

If the glue method of holding is being used, the timber must be planed flat in both cases, and when the paper joint is made both components must be squeezed in a vice. If the electric glue gun is being used (see page 31), restrict the size of the timber to 3½ in. (89 mm) diameter and 1¼ in. (32 mm) thickness. Again, the surfaces must be flat, only a thin film of glue used and, once more, both components squeezed in a vice to ensure adequate contact.

When boring tools are being used, particularly the long-hole boring auger for cutting the flex hole in desk and standard lamps, the long-hole boring adapter must replace the tee-rest and be securely placed in the dead centre recess in the timber. Feed the auger through the attachment and frequently withdraw it, so that the chips can be ejected. Failure to do this can result in complete blockage of the shell, burning of the bit itself and possibly bursting of the wood, or even the auger running off centre and emerging on the outside of the turning.

Where deep holes are being bored with tools like the sawtooth cutter, it is essential for the speed of the lathe to be related to the size of the hole being bored and for the rate of feed of the tool to be as fast as the machine will allow without slowing. This will avoid scorching of the shavings and wood dust, and possible drawing of the temper of the tool. Care must also be taken to ensure that the shavings will easily leave the hole, and it is wise to place the escapement of the bit so that it faces the bed of the lathe, thus assisting the fall-out of the shavings. When flatbits are in use, high speed is necessary and care must be taken here not to feed too fast, since there is the possibility of the bit running with the grain and consequently off centre. In all cases of boring, the tailstock must be firmly locked to the bed; a wise precaution is to feed the bit forward with the machine stopped so that the brad point can score the centre of the work, with the timber rotated by hand. All these tools should, of course, be sharp so that they can feed easily and avoid excessive weight being applied.

Care of the lathe

The bed of the lathe should be very carefully greased from time to time, particularly if it is to be left for long periods. The machining of the bed is of a very high order and any rust will seriously harm the surface and make the movement of the tailstock difficult. Keep the tailstock sleeve lubricated and the thread clean and lightly greased.

Grease cups should be kept topped up and screwed down from time to time to keep the bearings continuously lubricated, unless the lathe is fitted with sealed bearings.

Vacuum-clean the electric motor periodically to extract dust.

Check the belt tension regularly and replace a belt which may have become stretched or frayed.

Be sure that the pulleys are locked firmly to their shafts.

Keep metal tee-rests straight and true by an occasional rub with the file. Wooden rests should be planed accurately with a jack plane.

Keep the lathe centres in good condition; the dead centre should always be of perfect shape and the chisels of the driving fork sharpened from time to time with a smooth file. Never hammer the wood on to the driving fork centres, as this can damage the headstock bearings. An old driving fork can be driven into the timber, using a copper-headed hammer to provide centre and chisel holes.

Lightly oil all screw threads and keep them free from wood chips and dust. Keep components in a clean condition—the author has found it useful to protect them with a spray lacquer.

Examine all tool handles for security before use, because a loose handle coming away from the gouge or chisel in use can create a dangerous situation. By holding the blade and striking the end of the handle either on the bed of the lathe or on the floor, the security of the blade in the handle can be ensured.

Where the lathe is bolted to the floor, check the bolts occasionally for security. This is particularly important where large work is being undertaken.

Check the electrics, particularly the cable if it is not enclosed in conduit, to be sure that there is no fraying with the risk of the lathe becoming live in consequence.

Dust and the lathe

Dust is always something of a hazard and with some timbers it can have an irritating effect on the nostrils and can affect the skin. If the woodturner has any doubts about the suitability of any particular timber, he should make an enquiry to the Forest Products Research Laboratory or one of the governmental health departments to be quite sure. Timber such as mansonia can be quite harmful, and the author has had experience of extreme irritation from a timber called imbuia. (See page 67 for information concerning timbers injurious to health.)

To avoid dust of any sort, some woodturners favour a mask, although this can be quite uncomfortable particularly in a warm situation. Generally speaking, if timber is being cut there will be a minimum of dust, although some timbers fail to give a really nice shaving, the shaving breaking into a fine dust after leaving the tool. Excessive use of glasspaper creates a very dusty atmosphere, and it may be as well for the woodturner carrying out a great deal of this type of work to have readily available an industrial vacuum cleaner. This can be adapted to suck up the dust from the lathe bed and can, from time to time, be repositioned to remove the dust from elsewhere. Alternatively, he could design an extraction device to suit his particular lathe.

In schools and industrial undertakings there is now a growing insistence, due to the recent 'Safety at Work' Acts in various countries, to install dust-extracting equipment. However, this is extremely difficult to arrange for a tool like a lathe, where dust and shavings can be moving in almost any direction. The movement of dust is further aggravated by the running of the lathe itself. If the reader has any doubts about this, he should direct a question to the appropriate Factory Inspectorate.

3 The Beginner's Equipment

Choosing the lathe

The choice of lathe will largely depend upon the use to which it is to be put, whether for pleasure or production for profit, and upon the amount of running time and the cash available. The miniature lathes or the drill attachment lathes must be selected against size and capacity of finished product and, if the would-be woodturner intends to take up woodturning as a serious hobby, he would be well advised to opt for the professional lathe. There are any number to choose from at a wide range of cost.

Lathes are usually available with a choice of standard, short-bed or bowl-turning head only. The standard lathe is quoted as having a between-centres size. The short-bed lathe should accommodate at least 18 in. (460 mm) (chair leg size) between centres. The amateur would rarely consider a lathe having bowl-turning facilities only. Always take the manufacturers' advice in regard to the motor type and capacity suitable for their particular lathe. Manufacturers are usually prepared to supply approved safety switching for the electrics.

Standard equipment supplied with most lathes is as follows: driving fork centre, solid centre or cup-type centre for the tailstock, large outboard faceplate, inner faceplace, Morse taper centre drift, spanner to grip headstock spindle when removing screwed components, and long and short tee-rests.

Additional essential equipment

Faceplates

There are left-hand and right-hand faceplates, 3 in. (75 mm) diameter or 4 in. (100 mm) diameter. They are suitable for holding most discs for bowl and box work.

Collar or egg-cup chuck

These chucks are screwed to the nose of the headstock mandrel and are used for holding timber up to 2 in. (50 mm) diameter when making egg-cups, small boxes and serviette rings.

Screw-flange chuck

Select a chuck of this type with a removable and replaceable screw. This chuck can be used for holding timber of small diameter.

Tailstock drill chuck

A chuck having a Morse taper arbor to suit the tailstock mandrel and a capacity of ½ inch (13 mm) to suit the standard ½ in. machine shanks. This chuck is essential for holding sawtooth cutters and flatbits for deep-hole boring.

Universal chuck

One of these chucks will eliminate the need for either the collar or screw chuck. Rings supplied for use with this chuck will make the purchase of faceplates unnecessary.

Cutting tools

Cutting tools should include the following:

> Gouges, shallow section, 1, ½ and ¼ in. (25, 13, 6 mm)
> Gouges, deep-fluted, long and strong, ½ or ⅜ in. (13, 9 mm).
> Chisels, skew, 1 in. and ½ in. (25, 13 mm)
> Beading chisel, ¼ in. (6 mm)
> Parting tool
> Gouges, standard, deep-fluted, ¾ in. (19 mm)

On the other hand a beginner may care to invest in a manufacturers' standard set such as the Marples set of eight, No. M1002.

Additional tools can be added from time to time as skill increases or as a particular need arises. If the author's advice is taken in regard to the making of scraping chisels (see page 43), then these can be made from standard chisel blades.

For deep-hole boring, a set of Ridgway flatbits, ¼–1½ in. (6–38 mm) will be found ideal for general use.

Ridgway sawtooth cutters 2 in. (50 mm), 1¾ in. (44 mm) and 1½ in. (38 mm) would provide a lifetime of service in the boring of boxes, vases, etc.

A lamp standard long-hole boring auger, Ridgway R219, 30 × $^5/_{16}$ in. (762 × 7.9 mm), with a boring attachment recommended for the particular lathe and supplied by the lathe manufacturer, can be added if this type of work is envisaged.

A number of small-size wood twist drills will be needed; $^5/_{32}$ in. (3.95 mm), $^3/_{16}$ in. (4.8 mm), $^7/_{32}$ in. (5.55 mm), ¼ in. (6 mm), and $^5/_{16}$ in. (7.9 mm) would meet most cases.

Sharpening equipment

Sharpening equipment should be purchased for the sharpening of chisels and gouges.

A standard bench stone, India or carborundum 8 × 2 × 1 in. (200 × 50 × 25 mm), together with a slipstone 4 × 2 × ½ × ⅛ in. (100 × 50 × 13 × 3 mm), are essential basic requirements. Also a Cratex rubberized abrasive stick 6 × 1 × ⅜ in. (150 × 25 × 9.5 mm), fine grade, is required for final honing.

Useful aids

Most lathes are equipped with faceplates, driving forks and centres, but unfortunately these accessories seem to have been designed with large sections of timber in mind only. No provision is made for mounting small pieces of timber for work on the headstock, other than with the screw chuck. Thus, spindle-turning work below ¾ in. (19 mm) square has to be cut from timber above this size. To this end, it is suggested that several small attachments are made for the lathe.

A method often used to avoid screw holes in the work is to glue the workpiece to a block of wood previously screwed to the faceplate. To make final separation easy, a piece of paper is placed between the workpiece and the faceplate block. This, however, is wasteful of time and there is always the risk of splitting the finished workpiece when removing it, particularly where the base is thin.

Glue gun

A simpler method is to use a hot melt glue gun, without paper. The glue is melted by a small element in the gun and spread by means of the gun nozzle on to the block of wood screwed to the faceplate. Only a thin film of glue is required, and the workpiece is pressed into place (squeezed in a vice if possible). Turning can commence immediately. To remove the finished workpiece, a knife can be pushed into the joint. The glue remains on the glue chuck and can be re-melted for later use.

Fig. 3.1
Hot-melt glue gun

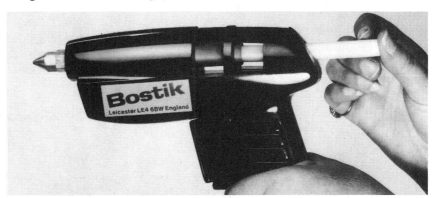

Fig. 3.2
Glueing small block on to the glue chuck

Mandrel

Alternatively, a mandrel can be turned between centres, with one end having a Morse taper to suit the particular lathe.

The face of the mandrel is turned flat and small pieces of timber to be turned are glued to this face, again by using the hot melt glue gun.

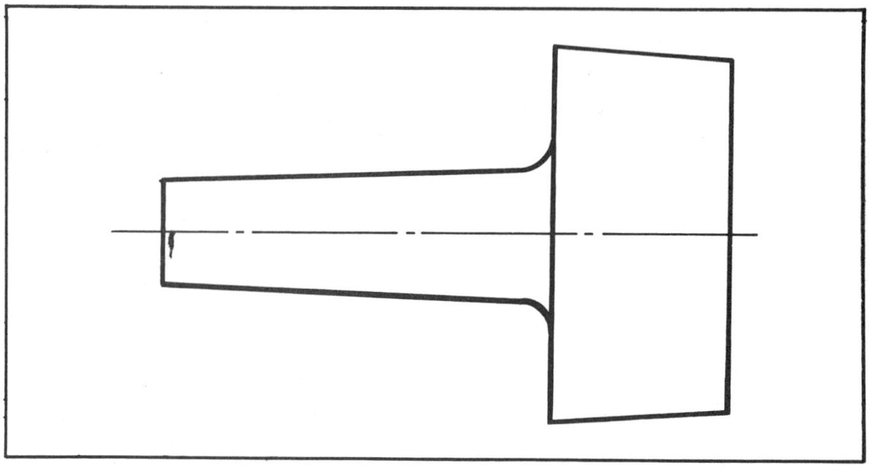

Fig. 3.3
Mandrel as glue chuck

To drive pieces of wood between centres requires a driving fork in the headstock, the other end of the wood being supported by the dead centre. Unfortunately, the average driving centre is too large to be used for small pieces. Cut a square pyramidal hole in the centre of a block of wood attached to the faceplate or use the mandrel with the Morse taper. Small square-section timber can be turned by inserting it into this hole. Slightly larger timber can be tapered at one end.

Fig. 3.4
Mandrels with square hole

Fig. 3.5
Pyramidal hole mandrel

Fig. 3.6
Pyramidal hole mandrel

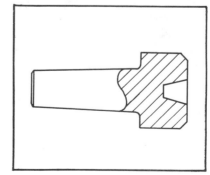
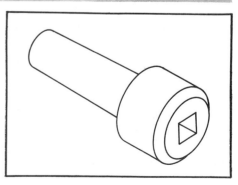

Another variation of the mandrel is to cut the head to a specific size, with a tiny taper front to back, to receive a pre-bored piece of wood which is to be made into a tiny frame or small box. The mandrel can also be recessed and then used as a wood chuck to receive tiny turned parts.

Morse taper

If metalturning facilities are available, a Morse taper can be fitted with various sized heads turned from aluminium alloy or other suitable metal. These have a slight taper with a recess cut to receive a disc of hardboard. When cutting through, as when making tiny picture frames, the hardboard will prevent the cutting edge from striking the metal. Alternatively, a piece attached to a faceplate can be recessed to receive a small turning.

Fig. 3.7
Taper mandrel

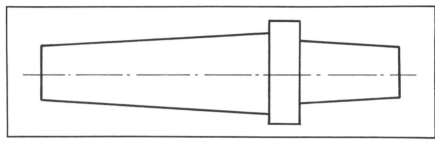

Fig. 3.8
Metal mandrel with removable heads

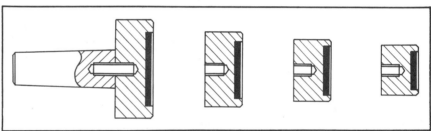

Fig. 3.9
Metal mandrel with removable heads

Fig. 3.10
Recessed chuck for small turnings

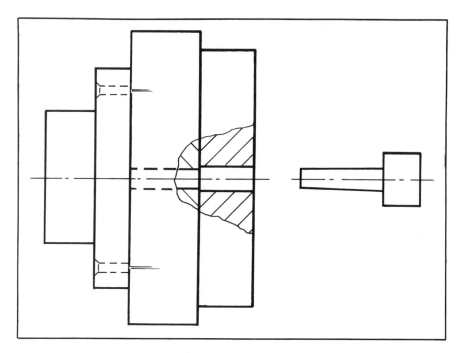

Types of mandrel

Egg-cup mandrel

This mandrel can be turned between centres. Cut a taper to suit the lathe, remove and test taper. Use a template to cut the mandrel to exact shape and size.

The egg-cup mandrel, with the taper fitted into the headstock, can be used for outside turning after boring the inside with a spade/flatbit.

It will be found useful for cleaning up and polishing or repolishing egg-cups.

Fig. 3.11
Egg-cup turning mandrel

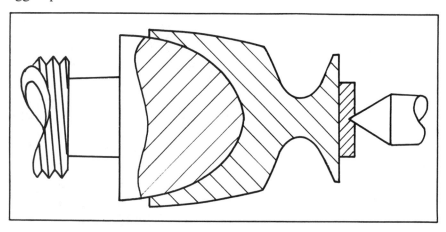

Cup chuck held taper mandrel

This is used to hold small boxes, lids and vases to facilitate the turning, shaping or cleaning up of the base after parting off.

Turn up between centres a piece of close-grained hardwood to the shape shown on the diagram and sized to suit the job in hand.

The taper on the cup chuck end should give a fairly tight fit and keep the centricity of the work during use. The working taper size will depend upon the work being turned.

It is suggested that a number of these mandrels be made to receive the most popular sizes.

Alternatively, a block of wood mounted on a faceplate can be taper-turned and small work held securely.

Fig. 3.12
Cup chuck held taper mandrel

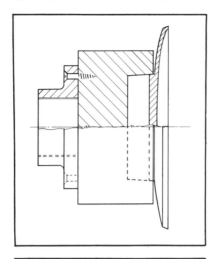

Fig. 3.13
Faceplate-mounted block—taper-turned

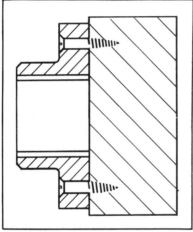

Taper mandrel

Serviette and other rings made by mounting the timber on the screw chuck or collar chuck are usually bored out using a sawtooth cutter, each ring being parted off a little, before the boring takes place.

After parting, the rings must be remounted for cleaning up the ends and polishing.

Fig. 3.14
Taper mandrel for serviette and other rings

Mount between centres a piece of close-grained hardwood, and turn it down to the appropriate sizes and taper.

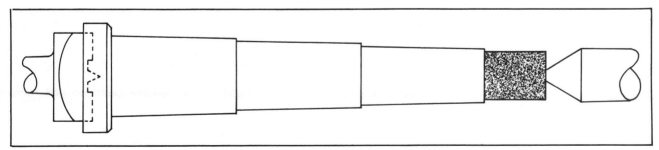

Chucks you can make

Adjustable chuck with jubilee clip adjustment

This chuck can be used to hold small boxes, vases and lids.

Fig. 3.15
Adjustable chuck with jubilee clip

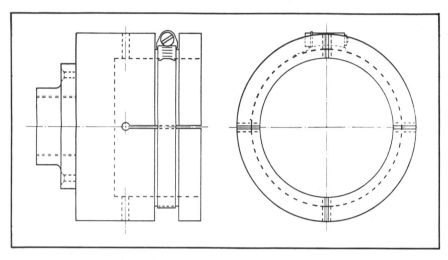

Mount a suitable block of wood on a 3 in. (75 mm) faceplate. Turn down to round, then cut a recess the required size and to a depth sufficient to receive the box.

Cut a groove near the face of the chuck, wide enough to receive a standard jubilee clip.

Remove the chuck from the lathe and, using a tenon saw, carefully make two saw kerfs at right-angles to each other, cutting at least two-thirds the depth of the previously turned recess.

Place a jubilee clip in the groove; when tightened, this will allow the sides of the chuck to be closed up on a disc placed in the chuck. The chuck will be particularly useful for repetition work, allowing for slight differences in diameter, and also permit take-up due to wear.

Fig. 3.16
Adjustable chuck with jubilee clip

Split chuck with squeeze collar

Mount a block of wood on a small faceplate. Turn to round, bore out and part off a collar of the dimensions given.

Bore out the block, using a bit of correct size, and cut slots with a saw at right-angles to each other to the depth indicated.

Replace the block on the lathe and turn down the outside tapering sufficiently to allow the collar to be pushed over the end.

A disc placed in the chuck can be securely held by pushing the collar along the taper, causing the saw slots to close.

Fig. 3.17
Split chuck with squeeze collar

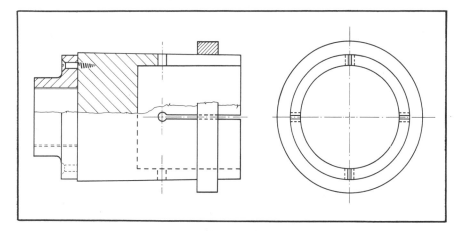

Fig. 3.18
Split chuck with squeeze collar

4 Tools for Woodturning

Cutting tools

Tools for woodturning can be grouped under three headings of style as well as of cutting. The styles are: long and strong, standard, and small standard.

Each of these styles can be divided into three group types—gouges, chisels and parting tools, and scraping chisels—while gouges can be further classified as shallow-fluted, deep-fluted long and strong, and deep-fluted standard.

The noses can be ground square across, or round like the shape of the end of the little finger.

Chisels are ground skew or square across.

Fig. 4.1
Round-nose gouge

Fig. 4.2
Deep-fluted gouge

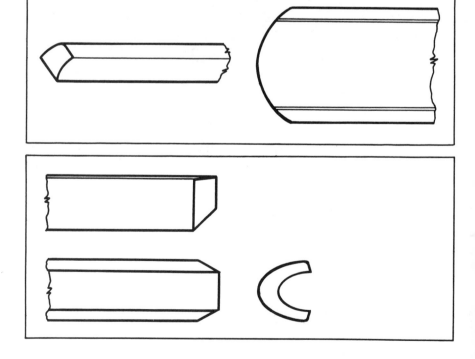

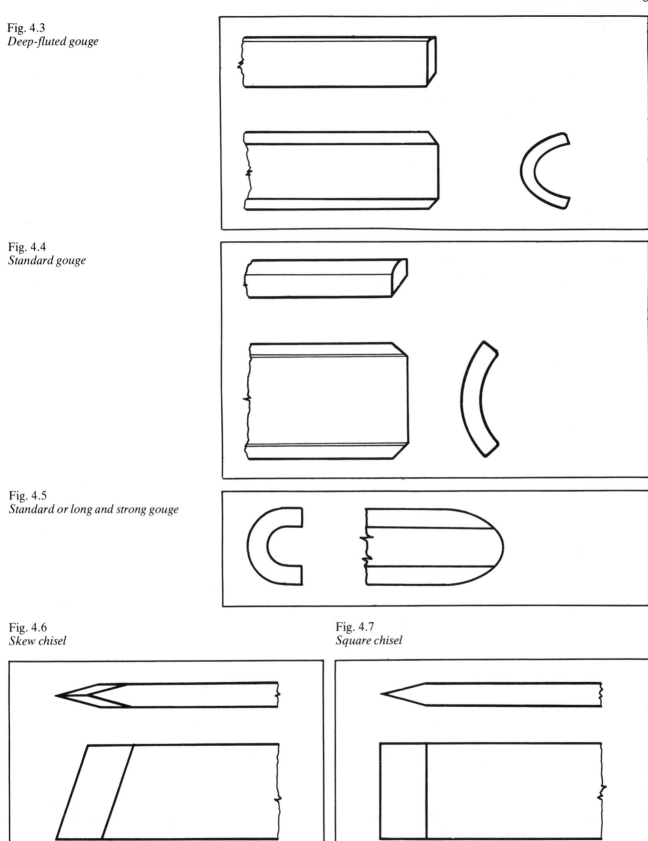

Fig. 4.3
Deep-fluted gouge

Fig. 4.4
Standard gouge

Fig. 4.5
Standard or long and strong gouge

Fig. 4.6
Skew chisel

Fig. 4.7
Square chisel

Scraping chisels

Scraping chisels are available in all three styles, and are ground on one side only in a variety of shapes chosen for different cutting applications.

Lathe work is divided into spindle work and faceplate work; in practice, most of the tools are not interchangeable.

Long and strong tools are usually over 18 in. (460 mm) in total length, with stout handles and thick blades. They have long been regarded as the tools for the professional, but are also strongly recommended for students in colleges and schools.

Standard tools are equally useful and can be used for most turning, apart from deep-bowl work.

For spindle turning

When roughing to size, many turners, particularly those with experience, use a standard length gouge but deep, either ¾ in. (19 mm) or 1¼ in. (32 mm) across, also ground square (see fig. 4.3).

Roughing between centres is best carried out with a long and strong shallow gouge 1 in. (25 mm) ground square across. This is an extremely safe tool for beginners (see fig. 4.4).

For coving

A standard or long and strong gouge can be used for coving, but the nose must be round like the end of the little finger (see fig. 4.5).

For planing

The 1 in. (25 mm) skew chisel is used for planing. Chisels can also be square across and are always ground on both sides. The chisel is also used for rounding, beading, tapering, and squaring shoulders (see figs 4.6 and 4.7).

For beading

Beading is usually carried out with a ¼ in. (6 mm) chisel, ground square across.

When marking out and parting off, a parting tool is used. This is a deep chisel ground on both sides and square across. It is tapered from front to back to give clearance for deep cutting. Some woodturners also use this tool for beading.

Fig. 4.8
Parting tool

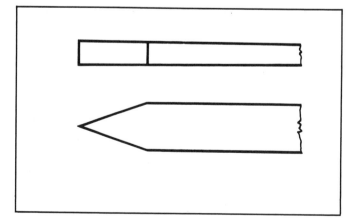

For faceplate work

Long and strong gouges, ground square across and deep, are used for faceplate work. The ⅜ in. and ½ in. (9.5 mm and 13 mm) sizes are best for bowl turning.

For smaller work, the spindle gouge with rounded nose ⅜ in. and ½ in. (9.5 and 13 mm) can be used. The ¼ in. (6 mm) will be found suitable for mini-turning.

The ¼ in. (6 mm) tool, made by Marples, is deeper than average and is probably the finest of its kind ever produced.

Scraping chisels in various shapes are used for cleaning up and improving.

Boring tools

Boring tools for the lathe can be classified into hand-held and chuck-held types. The latter are held in the drill chuck located in the tailstock.

Hand-held boring tool—the auger

The selection of the correct tools for particular jobs will go a long way towards ensuring perfection in lathe craftsmanship. Too often in the past, ignorance about hole-boring tools has been disastrous in effect.

The only tool designed purely with lathe hole boring in mind is the lamp standard shell auger (Ridgway R219). As its name indicates, this shell auger has been designed to cut easily into end grain, its central lip ensures the centricity of the bit, and long lengths of timber can be bored accurately to receive electric flex. The auger should be fitted with a cross-handle, which is not normally supplied with the auger. A suitable design for the handle is shown in the project section (chapter 12).

Fig. 4.9
Lamp standard shell auger

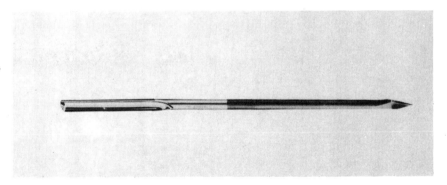

How the auger cuts

Unlike auger bits of the twist pattern type, which have a screw nose, the shell auger has to be pushed into the wood, the waste being removed through the shell form of the bit. Its nose comprises a cutting lip and cutter; the curve of the lip ensures that the auger runs centrally and is unaffected by the run of the grain or texture of the turning timber. The leading edge of the shell serves to smooth the hole and is relieved to prevent binding. Once penetration has started, the nose form leads the auger into the timber under normal pressure. With very hard timber, it may be necessary to pre-bore a starter hole, using a wood drill.

Chuck-held boring tools

Flatbits

The flatbit is of simple design, consisting of a long brad point to assist the boring of angled holes and forward and side cutting edges which together combine to give a spur-like cutting action on the periphery of the hole. All edges are therefore cutting edges and the hole is scraped or planed. Three flats on the shank give accurate placement of the bit in the three-jaw chuck and they are long enough to prevent any possibility of the jaws closing on the round shank of the bit.

The flatbit will fit any drill chuck held in the tailstock of the lathe. An extension facilitates the boring of deeper holes ⅝ in. (16 mm) and above in diameter.

The flatbit bores easily in both hardwood and softwood and requires a fast speed.

Sawtooth machine centre bit

This bit is probably the most useful boring tool which the woodturner can add to his kit. It will bore holes easily in hardwoods or softwoods having high or normal moisture content.

The sawtooth machine centre bit consists of a number of teeth, not unlike those of the ripsaw, around the periphery of the tool, together with two cutters or lifters and a small brad point. The saw teeth scribe and cut the circumference of the hole, and the cutter lifts and ejects the shavings. Sizes up to 3 in. (75 mm) diameter have a ½ in. × 2 in. (13 × 50 mm) shank. It bores shallow or deep holes accurately in face and end grain, in softwoods or hardwoods. Although of fairly light construction, it bores easily without overloading the machine and does not choke.

Fig. 4.10
Ridgway flatbit

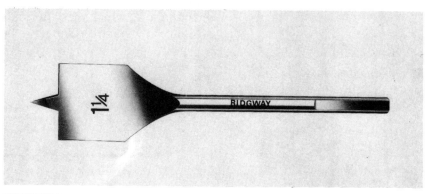

Fig. 4.11
Sawtooth machine centre bit

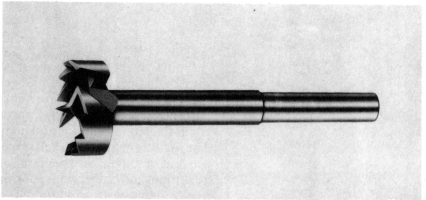

Forstner pattern machine bit

These bits consist of a double cutter and, although they have a small brad point, the bit actually runs on its circular rim.

A unique bit, it is designed to cut any arc of a circle perfectly in hardwood or softwood and its direction is unaffected by coarse grain or knots. The holes are accurate to size, and are clean and flat-bottomed. It is ideal for cutting shallow holes in thin timber, overlapping holes or holes at close centres.

Fig. 4.12
Forstner pattern machine bit

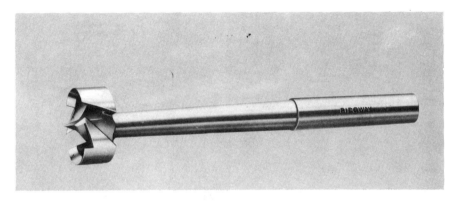

Wood drill and lip and spur drills

These drills cut a fine hole in the face and end grain of hardwood or softwood. Available in small sizes, wood drills are particularly useful for boring the tiny holes in condiment and sugar pots.

The drills are assembled in the tailstock chuck, and the speeds outlined in the table of boring speeds (see page 73) should be observed.

Fig. 4.13
Wood drill

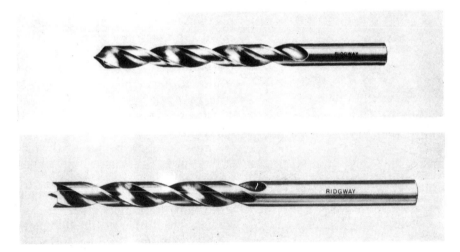

Fig. 4.14
Lip and spur drill

Woodturning tools you can make

Making scraping chisels

Scraping chisels, or scrapers, can be made from the standard woodturning chisel by re-grinding it to the desired shape. The reader is advised not to convert old files or other tools since these may be made from the wrong steel and will most certainly not have the correct temper. The five basic types of scraping chisel are described later (page 45).

These tools should be sharpened in the same way as the cabinet scraper, using a ticketer or burnisher. The ground angle can be between 85 deg. and 75 deg. included angle. They are used like the bench scraper; the forward tilt of the scraper on the bench is interpreted on the lathe by allowing the scraping chisel to 'trail', thus working slightly below centre.

Fig. 4.15
In scraping, the tool trails.

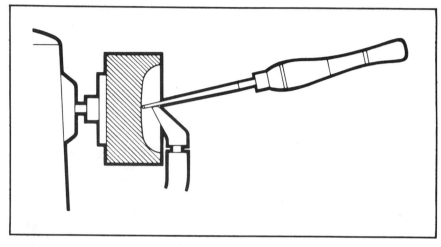

Fig. 4.15a
Template for 'setting piece,' 6" diameter wheel (shown here 40 percent of actual size)

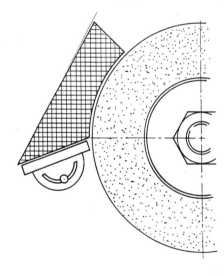

Sharpening scraping chisels

Grinding. Maintain the original shape. Adjust the table of the grinder close to the wheel, to give the correct angle. A 'setting piece' is an accurate way to do this. The setting piece not only saves time, but saves overgrinding and prevents overheating by reducing the amount of metal to be removed.

Swing the tool around on the table, following the tool shape. Remove as little metal as possible. Use light pressure to avoid burning.

Honing. Lay the scraper on the bench and remove the burr on the face of the tool with an oilstone slip. Hold the scraper on a tee-rest and hone the bevel lightly, taking great care not to 'dub-over' (this action will produce a very fine burr which will be ideal for use on box, ebony and other close-grained hardwoods. For coarser grained woods, again remove this burr by honing the face. This should leave a keen edge, free from snags or nicks.

Ticketing. Use, for preference, a ticketer of the type shown or a $^3/_{16}$ in. (4.5 mm) hardened silver steel rod. Burnish the top face of the tool, taking great care not to tilt the ticketer. This action merely 'consolidates' the edge. Holding the tool in the left hand, close to the body, feel the bevel with the ticketer, raise it a degree or two and with plenty of pressure turn back the edge of the scraper to form the burr which does the cutting.

Making a ticketer

Use an old 4 in. (100 mm) triangular (three-square) file and grind the teeth away. Grind a small radius on the corners and polish all over with oil and emery cloth. Fit a good-quality handle, ensuring that the tang is a tight fit.

Fig. 4.16
Ticketer

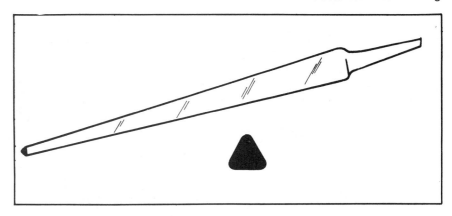

The basic types of scraping chisel

For a wide range of work the reader is advised to grind five basic scraping chisels. Use standard 1 in. (25 mm) turning chisel blades.

Hollowing scraper

For general roughing work such as hollowing and shaping, a tool with a round nose, as illustrated, is suitable for following most curves. It can be used on work mounted either on the left- or right-hand side of the headstock. Also illustrated are various uses of the tool.

Fig. 4.17
Hollowing scraper

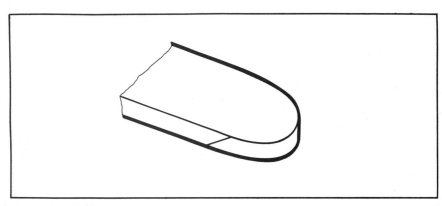

Fig. 4.18
Scraping an egg-cup

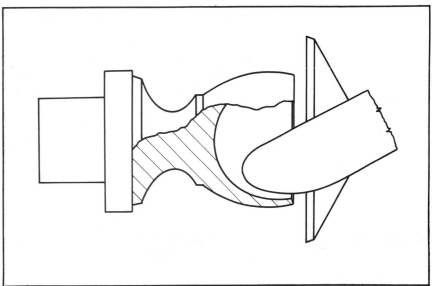

Fig. 4.19
Scraping on left-hand side of the headstock

Fig. 4.20
Scraping on right-hand side of the headstock

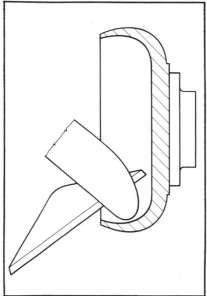
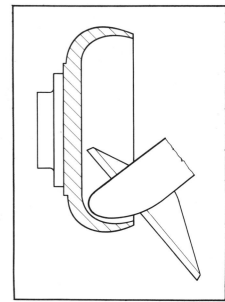

Flatting scraper

For fine finishing and flatting, the flatting scraper can be used in either the right- or left-hand lathe position. The illustrations show the flatting scraper in use.

Fig. 4.22
Scraping on the left-hand side of the lathe

Fig. 4.21
Flatting scraper

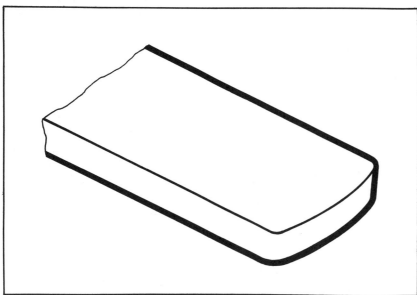

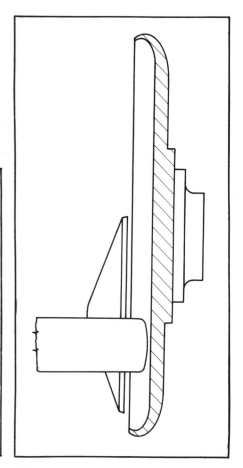

Fig. 4.23
Scraping on the left-hand side of the lathe

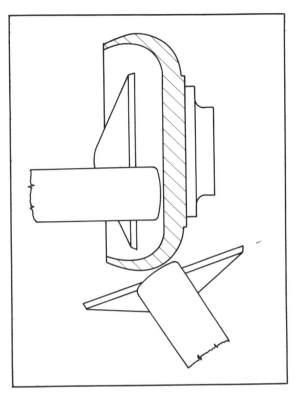

Backing scraper

This tool is shaped to cut the base of a turning, mounted at either end of the headstock. Its edge is shaped to permit the tool to be used in the narrow space between the headstock and the job mounted on the face-plate. Its point can also be used as a vee-tool for marking out, or cutting a point of start. Some uses of the backing scraper are illustrated.

Fig. 4.24
Backing scraper

Fig. 4.25
Backing at right-hand side of lathe

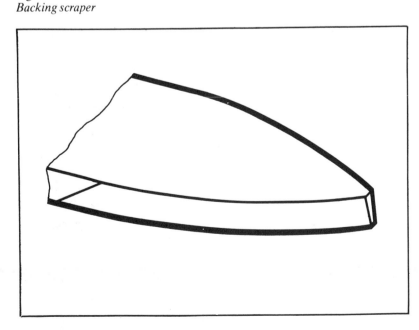

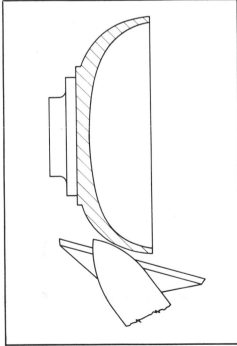

Fig. 4.26
Backing at left-hand side of lathe

Fig. 4.27
Cutting point of start

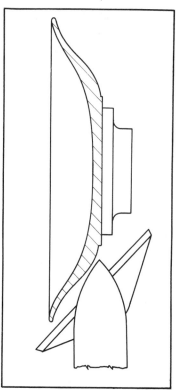

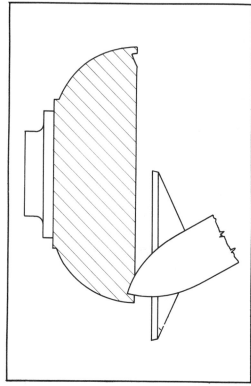

Left- and right-hand spades

The spade is used for trimming the sides and bottoms, particularly of square boxes and other work. It has two cutting edges, the included angle between which is less than 90 deg. to permit the tool to be used in a square corner but with only one edge cutting. This prevents any tendency of the tool to snatch. Illustrations show the tool in use.

Fig. 4.28
Left-hand spade

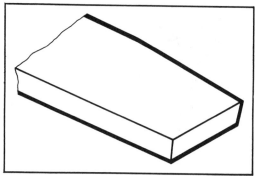

Fig. 4.29
Right-hand spade

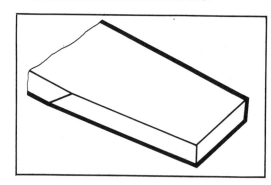

Fig. 4.30
Left-hand side of lathe—trimming the edge

Fig. 4.31
Left-hand side of lathe—scraping the side

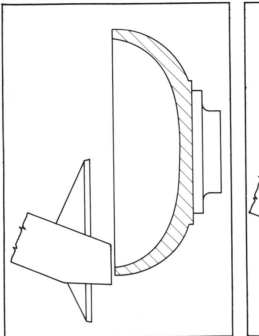

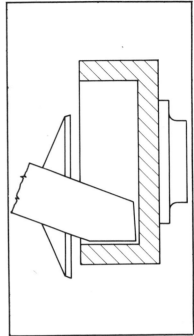

Fig. 4.32
Right-hand side of lathe—trimming the outside

Fig. 4.33
Right-hand side of lathe—cutting a recess; dotted lines, trimming the bottom

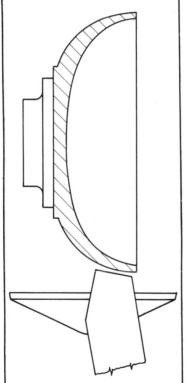

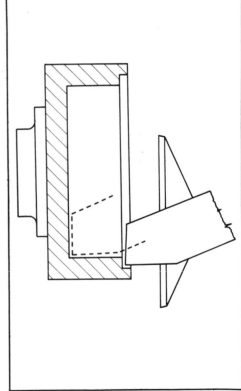

5 Sharpening and Sharpening Equipment

Stones

Sharpening stones are available in two types—manufactured stones of artificial grits and natural stones quarried from deposits of novaculite rock in the State of Arkansas, USA.

Perhaps the best known of the manufactured stones is the world-famous Norton, made from alundum (aluminium oxide). This abrasive is produced in an electric furnace, giving the accuracy with which uniformity can be maintained in regard to grit-size cutting properties with consistent hardness and texture throughout the stone. These oilstones are also presaturated with oil before leaving the factory; thus, they hold a pool of oil which is not immediately soaked up by the stone, allowing particles of steel to float away and preventing the stone from being clogged and glazed. These stones are available in fine, medium and coarse grades. Bench stones are also available as combination stones, with one side fine and the other coarse.

Arkansas stones are capable of producing the finest edge and are available in the following four grades. (1) Washita, which is perhaps the best known and fastest cutting stone, although it is of fairly coarse texture. (2) Soft Arkansas, which can be used for sharpening most tools. (3) Hard Arkansas, which is regarded as a finishing stone to be used after first sharpening on a coarser grade stone; sharpening takes longer but the edge is a fine one. (4) Black Hard Arkansas, which is the ultimate in sharpening stones. It is used only to add perfection to an already sharpened edge.

A recent addition to the man-made stones giving an edge equivalent to the Black Hard, is the Ultimate Diemond Stone, manufactured by the Brenner Co., Ohio, USA. This is said never to wear, so it should last a lifetime.

Rubberized abrasives are becoming increasingly popular. They are sold in various shapes and sizes, and a range of grit grades is available in each shape. Rubberized wheels are extremely useful for tool grinding.

All these stones are extremely expensive and should be handled and used with great care.

The woodturner will need a bench stone, preferably a 6 or 8 × 2 × 1 in. (150 or 200 × 50 × 25 mm) Washita or India of the combination type.

A slipstone 4 × 2 × ½ × ⅛ in (100 × 50 × 13 × 3 mm) will meet most problems in gouge work.

A rubberized abrasive stick 6 × 1 × ⅜ in. (150 × 25 × 10 mm), fine grade, will serve to produce a fine edge with a polished bevel.

Files

For sharpening boring tools, a number of small files will be found useful. A set of needle files, taper flat, half-round, three-square, knife, square and round, having a cut number 2, i.e. an extra smooth cut, will meet most needs. The cut number is usually indicated on the knurled round handle.

Oils

The selection of a suitable oil for use on the oilstones is important. A thin oil of the three-in-one variety will do, but sweet oil or neatsfoot oil would be more suitable. Any oil which could dry on the stone and clog should be avoided.

Methods of sharpening the tools

All woodturning tools, when leaving the manufacturers, are accurately ground to correct angle and shape. Before using, they must be sharpened.

The golden rule of sharpening for turning tools is to sharpen on the ground bevel, since these tools do not have a sharpening bevel like the joiner's chisel used on the bench. They are best sharpened on a medium oilstone and for preference a polished finish should be arrived at; indeed, a buffed finish is the ultimate and it is this sort of finish which will be reflected in the turned timber, producing a surface which should not require abrasives of any kind.

The gouge

To sharpen the gouge, rest it on the ground bevel and move it backwards and forwards along the whole length of the stone, at the same time rolling it from side to side.

Fig. 5.1
Sharpen gouge on ground bevel

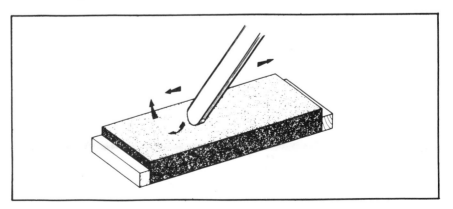

51

A perfect bevel finish can finally be achieved by carefully rotating the gouge, holding it at right-angles to the stone and moving it lengthwise along the stone.

This action will produce a wire edge on the inside of the gouge. Remove the wire edge with a slipstone, carefully keeping the slipstone flat as it moves through the flute. Maintain the original shape and the balance of the curve.

Fig. 5.2
Sharpening—finishing lengthways along stone

The ultimate finish can be obtained by polishing the bevel on a hard felt buff, using a proprietary brand of polishing compound. Alternatively, a rubberized abrasive wheel, substituted for the standard wheel on the electric grinder, will give a superb final finish to edge and bevel.

Fig. 5.3
Removing the wire edge

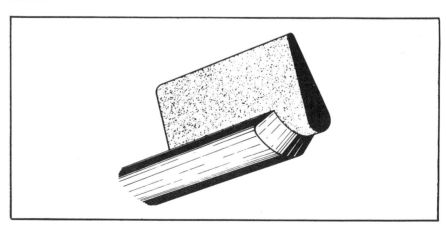

The chisel

Rest the ground bevel flat on the oilstone and move the chisel forward in a figure-of-eight movement along the whole length of the stone. The figure-of-eight movement will distribute the wear throughout the length and width of the stone. Carry out the sharpening of both bevels; the sharpening of the opposite side will automatically remove the wire edge thrown up on the first ground bevel. The parting tool can be sharpened in exactly the same way.

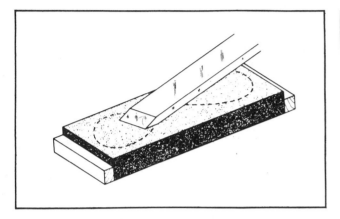

Fig. 5.4
Sharpen on both ground bevels—keep the bevels flat

Fig. 5.5
Sharpening the parting tool—sharpen parting tool on ground faces

Scrapers

Scraping chisels are ground at between 85 and 75 deg. included angle and on one side only.

The flat side of the scraping chisel, i.e. the top side when the scraping chisel is in use, should be absolutely flat and the bevel smooth. Arrive at this condition by rubbing the chisel on an oilstone if necessary.

Fig. 5.6
Sharpening the scrapers

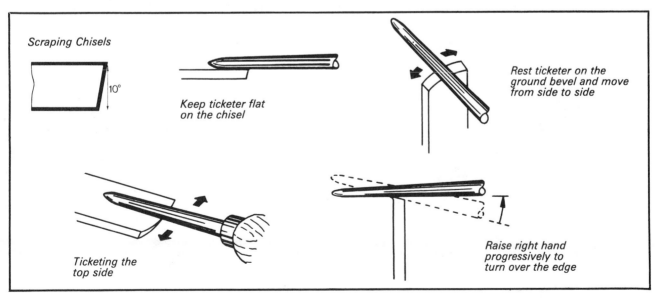

Scraping Chisels

10°

Keep ticketer flat
on the chisel

Rest ticketer on the
ground bevel and move
from side to side

Ticketing the
top side

Raise right hand
progressively to
turn over the edge

The scraping chisel is not sharpened like normal edge tools; it is first burnished and then a cutting edge is formed by pushing the edge over to form a burr or hook.

A small piece of hard round steel fitted in a file or chisel handle can be used as a burnisher or ticketer, but, as previously suggested, a 4 in. (100 mm) file with its teeth ground away and with its corners rounded makes a much better tool.

Place the tool flat on the bench, bevel side down, draw the burnisher along the edge, forward and back, pressing quite hard but making sure all the time that the burnisher lies dead flat on the blade. Do this enough times to consolidate the metal; this will give a tougher surface.

Now set up the chisel in a vice, with the ground edge towards the operator and with the burnisher lying flat on the ground bevel. Burnish to and fro, again pressing quite hard. As the burnishing proceeds, raise the handle by easy stages until the burnisher becomes almost horizontal. This sets up a burr or hook and the tool will be ready for use.

Alternatively, a hook can be formed simply by hard-burnishing, using the ticketer quite flat on the bevel. Avoid bringing the hook too far over.

The lamp standard shell auger

Considerable care must be exercised, when sharpening this tool, not to remove too much metal at the nose.

Hold the auger vertical in a vice. Use a dead-smooth flat or knife-edge file, keep the file flat on the lip of the nose and with great care make two or three strokes. This should generally be sufficient to restore the cutting edge. Check that the centre clearance is not obstructed; if necessary, draw the knife-edge file through to remove any burr.

Hold the auger horizontally in a vice to sharpen the shell edges. Use a slipstone of suitable radius, lightly oil and move it forward inside the shell, twisting it to the left so that the leading edge of the auger is whetted, as in the diagram.

Never sharpen the outside, otherwise the clearance will be lost and the auger will tend to bind in the hole. Never grind the lamp standard auger.

Fig. 5.7
Sharpening the lamp standard shell auger

Fig. 5.8
Sharpening the flatbit

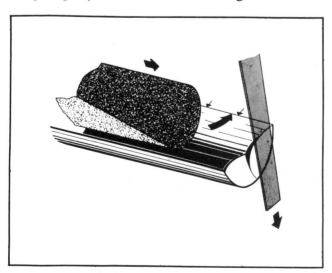

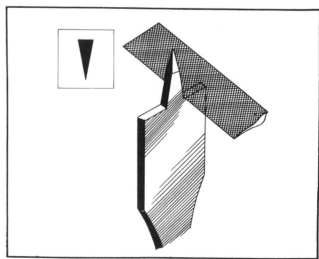

The flatbit

Secure the bit in a split block held in the vice. Use a knife-edge dead-smooth file or a small triangular stone.

Sharpen the forward cutting edges carefully, maintaining the original angles and keeping the ground surface flat. Sharpen equally and check the levels. Sharpen the brad point if necessary, maintaining the centricity of the point—again, sharpen both sides equally.

Use the file sparingly and do not oversharpen. Carefully maintain the shape and angles of the bit and never sharpen the sides of the bit, otherwise the effective diameter will be reduced.

The sawtooth machine bit

Secure the cutter in a block of wood held in a vice. Use a flat file, working through the throat of the bit to sharpen the lifters. Maintain the identical angle and keep the cutting edge straight.

Use a triangular saw file to file the teeth, maintaining the level of the teeth points around the periphery.

The brad point will rarely need attention but should sharpening be needed, file sparingly with a flat file, taking care to ensure its centricity.

Never file the lifter on the top or outer periphery of the bit. Never grind the tool by hand.

The Forstner bit

Secure the cutter in a block of wood held in a vice. Use a flat smooth file to sharpen the lifters, working through the throat of the cutter. Maintain the original sharpening angle and keep the edge straight. Remove as little metal as possible. (See previous notes and diagram on sharpening sawtooth machine bits.)

Use a round-edged slipstone to stone the inside of the rim; use a continuous rotary action to maintain the curve. Never stone the outside of the rim.

Fig. 5.10
Sharpening the Forstner machine bit

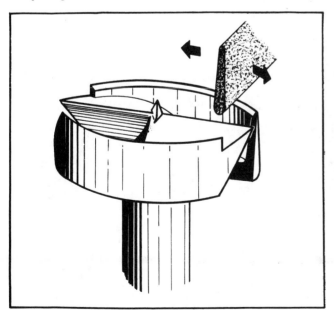

Fig. 5.9
Sharpening the sawtooth machine bit

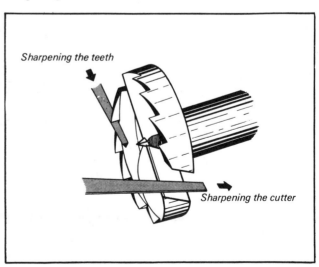

Sharpening the teeth

Sharpening the cutter

Fig. 5.11
Sharpening the Forstner machine bit

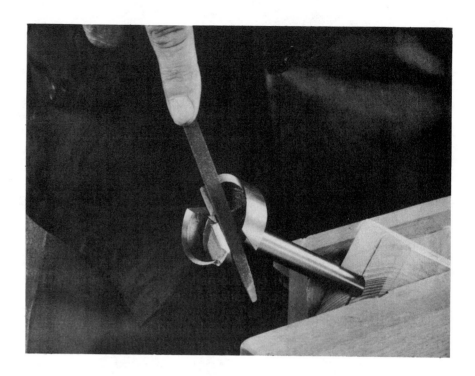

Fig. 5.12
Sharpening the lip and spur twist drill

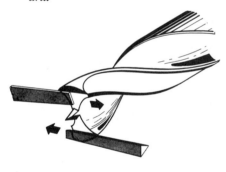

Fig. 5.13
Sharpening straight-shank twist drills

Lip and spur twist drills

Use a smooth flat file to sharpen both the spurs and the cutters. Keep the file flat and take off as little metal as possible.

The brad point should only very occasionally require attention. Take care to retain its centricity. Keep both pairs of cutters and spurs at the same height.

Straight-shank twist drills

The nose only is sharpened. This is best done on a grinding wheel using the side face, as in grinding a twist drill for metal. Maintain the special nose angle and the cutting edge relief. Be careful to keep the tool cool. Do not overheat to draw the temper.

6 Grinding and Grinding Equipment

All turning tools require grinding from time to time. Grinding will be needed for various reasons: (1) the cutting edge may be badly 'nicked'; (2) the ground bevel may, over a period of sharpening, become too short or rounded; (3) the tool may have lost its original shape. There are several types of equipment for grinding turning tools: (a) the dry grinder; (b) the Sharpedge (oil-cooled grinder); (c) the Sharpenset (water-cooled grinder); (d) the combined grinder/sharpener.

Grinding on the dry grinder

The grinder shown has a 6 in. (150 mm) diameter wheel, 1 in. (25 mm) thick and runs at about 3000 r.p.m. The wheel requires to be kept free from blemishes, smooth patches and clogged areas, and a wheel dresser is a necessity to dress the wheel regularly.

Fig. 6.1
The dry grinder

Fig. 6.2
Sharpedge oil-cooled grinder

Fig. 6.3
*Japanese waterstone
sharpening machine*

Fig. 6.4
The dry grinder—grinding the gouge

It is vitally necessary to keep the wheel in tip-top condition to ensure light easy grinding and to avoid pushing the tool hard upon the stone, causing overheating and burning of the steel.

A jar of cold water should be available so that the tool may be kept cool by frequent dipping.

Grind on the face of the stone, never on the side. This latter point cannot be overemphasized. Safety is to be kept constantly in mind. Place the gouge vertically and rest it on the tool rest so that the heel of the ground bevel rubs the stone. Roll the gouge from side to side and slowly raise the handle. Watch the line of light as the tool rolls over; this should move slowly towards the edge as the tool handle is progressively

Fig. 6.5
Elu MWA 149 sharpening
and honing machine

raised. Stop grinding the moment before the line of sparks (light) reaches the edge. This requires some practice, and great care must be taken not to overheat the tool to draw the temper and ruin it. Keep the ground angle of 40 deg. for gouges. The tool must now be sharpened on the oilstone.

Dry grinders having rubberized abrasive wheels are growing in popularity. Ideally, they should rotate away from the operator. A number of grits are available and they produce a perfect edge for the woodturner. A fine wheel will obviate the need for the sharpening stone, apart from the removal of the wire edge on the inside of the gouge, using a slip-stone or abrasive stick.

Grinding on the oil-cooled grinder

If a Denford Sharpedge is available, the turner may quickly produce a perfectly ground gouge without risk of overheating, since the tool is cooled by a constant flow of pumped oil moving across the stone, which is lying horizontally.

Rest the gouge at the correct angle on the stone, then roll it from side to side at the same time moving it across the rotating stone to distribute the wear evenly.

Fig. 6.6
Grinding on the Sharpedge

The Sharpedge produces a fairly fine finish on the bevel and it is possible to use the tool straight from the stone, although ideally it should be sharpened.

The horizontal grindstone is perfect for chisel grinding; the bevels are kept flat without the difficulty experienced with hollow grinding on the dry grinder.

Linishing belts

Linishing belts substituted for sanding belts on a belt sanding machine or discs of linishing quality (grit size 120), glued to a wooden disc attached to a faceplate, can be used as a substitute for a grinder. There is little danger of burning, especially if the machine can be run at a fairly low speed.

Fig. 6.7
Grinding the chisel on the linisher

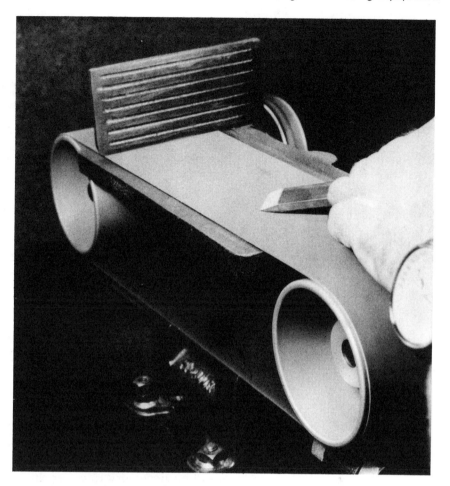

Dressing equipment

After a period of use, the grinding wheel will need to be dressed. This can be carried out by using one of the several types of rotating steel wheel dressers or a diamond wheel dresser.

Rubberized wheels can be cleaned by using a piece of coarse abrasive paper. Dressing must be carried out with great care to avoid waste.

7 Timbers Suitable for Woodturning

Choice of timbers

Most timbers can be successfully turned, but the choice of timber will often depend upon the use to which the turned article is to be put.

Domestic woodware in the UK was predominantly turned from sycamore, particularly in Wales. Contemporary fruitware and saladware uses a great deal of teak, although elm is preferred in the cheaper article.

Certainly, most of the hardwoods grown in Europe turn well and many have beautifully marked grain and superb colour. The following notes are not meant to be exhaustive; indeed, a separate large volume would be necessary to cover this aspect of the craft.

Ash *(Fraxinus excelsior)*

Ash provides a very tough and elastic timber without the hardness of oak. The timber is whitish grey, often with brown, yellow or pink markings. It seasons well and produces quite large sizes. It polishes well and turns easily, the turning often accentuating the beauty of the grain.

Beech *(Fagus sylvatica)*

Beech is the timber usually associated closely with woodturning. It is the tree of the Chiltern pole lathe turners and has long been associated with the furniture makers.

It grows to large size, is reddish brown in colour, with small medullary ray flecks. Its grain is straight and close. It has very few knots and seasons well. The northern European beeches are the harder. Turns extremely well, although its grain lacks attraction.

Chestnut *(Castanea sativa)*

There are two main types—sweet and Spanish. It looks a little like oak without the marked silver grain (medullary ray).

It is light brown in colour and it turns well, being softer than oak, and takes a very good finish. Obtainable in large sizes.

Elm *(Ulmus procera)*

This wood is in plentiful supply due to an excessively high felling programme brought about by the rapid spread of Dutch Elm disease.

The grain is fairly open, the timber dull reddish brown in colour. It turns well, both wet and dry; it is fairly hard and occasionally it is difficult to bring to a smooth finish from the tool. Excellent for domestic and other turnery.

Sycamore *(Acer pseudoplatanus)*

Often referred to as the great maple, the timbers are also somewhat alike. It grows to very good size, is creamy white in colour and has an attractive smooth grain. The medullary ray is often visible and gives an attractive ripple. The wood is fairly hard and heavy, strong and stable.

Care is needed during seasoning to avoid staining. The timber turns really well and is ideal for domestic woodware.

Yew *(Taxus baccata)*

This is an often much-despised tree, since it tends to have a fluted trunk and many flaws. It grows to a great age, but felled trunks tend to be wasteful and unproductive of large planks free from flaws.

It is extremely hard, with good grain, and its attractive colours range from orange reds through golden yellows to golden browns. Its dark summer rings enhance the grain enormously.

Turns extremely well and gives an excellent finish from the tool.

The foregoing are just a few of the commercially viable timbers; those that follow are fine for small turned work but are rarely on sale, so the turner would have to consider converting and seasoning for himself.

Apple *(Malus pumila, M. communis or M. pyrus)*

Again, this is rarely available in large sizes, but it provides a most pleasing timber. It is reddish brown in colour with attractive grain. The wood is fairly hard and tough, turns well and takes polish successfully.

Blackthorn *(Prunus spinosa)*

This is sometimes referred to as the wild plum—the sloe. It grows freely in the hedgerow, but rarely to large size. The timber has an extremely attractive reddish brown heartwood with yellow sapwood. Turns well.

Box *(Buxus sempervirens)*

Box is an extremely slow-growing tree, rarely found in large sizes. It is butter yellow in colour, the smaller sizes having many small knots. It is extremely hard and it turns with surprising ease, leaving a finely polished surface. Traditionally, this is the timber for the best chisel handles. It is useful for the smaller turned articles.

Cherry *(Prunus)*

There are many varieties, among them being *P. avium* the wild cherry. Some fair-sized timber is often available. It is reddish brown in colour and often has green and pinkish yellow tinges.

The wood is fairly hard, tough and strong, with an even texture. It turns extremely well, its interesting grain often enhancing the design of the turned work.

Hawthorn *(Crataegus monogyna)*

This is another tree of the hedgerow, although large specimens can be found growing freely in parkland. The timber is close grained but somewhat unattractive. White to yellow fawn in colour, its turning qualities are similar to those of box.

Holly *(Ilex aquifolium)*

Holly grows freely as ornamental trees and is also found in the hedgerow. Although large specimens have been felled, the tree is generally small. When properly converted, it should yield extremely white timber, although generally it tends towards a whitish green/grey. It is close grained, turns extremely well, takes polish easily and gives a lasting and pleasing finish straight from the tool.

Pear *(Pyrus communis)*

This may often be found growing to great height. It is pinkish brown in colour without marked grain, and is fairly hard and tough. It turns well and, since it has few knots, it is ideal for domestic woodware.

Plum *(Prunus domestica)*

Plum rarely grows to a large size. It is purple brown in colour with yellow striped sapwood, and has hard close grain of even texture. Like all the fruit trees, it turns well.

Alternative timbers

Other timbers suitable for woodturning but growing increasingly rare are walnut, oak, maple, hornbeam, plane, and service tree.

Timbers growing outside Europe and suitable for woodturning are many and various. The woodturner may find the following an attractive selection:

1. African walnut
2. Afrormosia
3. Australian silky oak
4. Greenheart
5. Honduras mahogany
6. Imbuia (Brazilian walnut)
7. Laurel
8. Lignum vitae
9. Mansonia
10. Olivewood
11. Padauk
12. Purpleheart
13. Rosewood
14. Teak
15. Utile

Timbers generally available on the American market and suitable for woodturning are:

1. American black walnut
2. Brazilian rosewood
3. Bubinga
4. Butternut
5. Cherry
6. Lignum
7. Maple
8. Oak
9. Padauk
10. Purpleheart
11. Teak
12. Walnut
13. Zebrawood

Seasoning the timbers

It is quite possible to season some timbers by leaving them in the log, but with timbers such as apple and cherry it is highly desirable for these to be converted as soon as possible. The person who knows exactly the purpose for which the timber is required is fortunate and will be able to decide the thicknesses to which the log can be sawn. If the log is large, he may saw it straight through the middle and then take the advantage, for example, if it has an agreeable medullary ray, to saw it radially.

Sawing the log into planks will obviously quicken the drying. Planks should be stacked with stickers in between to give the maximum flow of air around each plank. These stickers are best made of hardwood and should be between ½ in. (13 mm) and 1 in. (25 mm) square, depending on the type of timber being seasoned. They should first of all be laid on battens on the ground at approximately 1 ft (300 mm) distances apart. The planks are laid one on top of the other and each sticker placed exactly and immediately above the other.

Generally, it is wise to place heavy weights on the last plank and to cover the top of the stack with a protective plank or possibly a tarpaulin cover, but on no account should the sides or the ends of the planks be covered. Every precaution should be taken to avoid heavy rain soaking the stack and, with some timbers like holly or sycamore which may discolour, it is necessary to place the stack in a protective shed of an open-sided variety.

The period of seasoning will vary, depending upon the thickness of the planks and the size of the actual trees, but after about six months with smaller trunks it may be possible to move the timber into a cool building and after a few weeks into the workshop.

If means of conversion are not immediately to hand, it would be wise to split each log down the centre using wedges. This will prevent the log from uneven drying and shakes will be reduced.

Air-seasoned timber will have a moisture content of approximately 18 per cent, compared with that of kiln-dried timber which is between 10 and 12 per cent.

Air seasoning will take approximately one year per inch of thickness, as against a kiln-drying period of 1–3 weeks per inch (25 mm).

P.E.G. seasoning

This is a method of seasoning increasing in use all over the world. P.E.G. is a wax-like material which dissolves in water, and is in fact polyethylene glycol 1000.

The wood is turned green and soaked for a period of time. An action called osmosis takes place, whereby the sap is replaced by the polyethylene glycol. After soaking, the wood is dried in a warm workshop. The period of drying depends on the thickness of the stack.

Seasoning timbers from the garden and hedgerow

Most of the timbers growing in gardens in the UK, and which may be seen growing in hedgerows and spinneys, can be used for woodturning. Certainly, many of them are far more beautiful in grain and colour than the much-lauded imported timbers. Fruit trees such as the apple and the cherry are most beautiful and, indeed, many of the timbers commonly found in the hedgerow, like the hawthorn, the blackthorn and the holly, although not giving large-size trunks, do provide the most attractive and wholly satisfying timber.

Apple

Apple is a very slow-drying timber and great care needs to be taken in its seasoning to prevent it splitting or severely warping. Many of the logs tend to twist in growth and, if the log is not converted immediately, spiral splits around the trunk may well render it useless. The logs should be converted quickly and preferably into finalized thicknesses which the user can envisage being used on his lathe. It is preferable to seal the ends of each plank and, if necessary, tack on a lath. Sealing is best carried out by painting with liquid paraffin wax, but ordinary paint can be used; indeed, this is the method often used by sawmills. The boards should be stacked with 1 in. (25 mm) square stickers between them and, when stacking, be sure that air can move completely round the stack. Whenever possible, the bark should be left on the tree during the first half of the drying period. Very large trunks may well have rotted hearts and, if such a trunk is converted, it is advisable to remove the rot immediately. Always weight the stack and cover at the top to prevent discoloration by rain.

Beech

The beech tree, unlike fruit trees, dries fairly rapidly and requires very little attention in regard to the protection of its ends with paraffin wax or laths. Usually, beech trees are felled in the early winter months and, because of the possibility of attack by insects, it is as well to strip off the bark. Again, the stack should be weighted fairly heavily. Remember that home-converted beech will tend to be rather pale in colour, unlike commercial beech which is generally steamed and is a reddish pink in colour.

Cherry

Cherry provides a very acceptable woodturning timber. It requires to be sawn immediately upon felling and the stickers should be a little less in thickness than those for apple, i.e. approximately ¾ in. (19 mm). The stack should be heavily weighted, since cherry has a marked tendency to twist and warp.

Holly

Holly gives us the whitest known timber in the UK. It should be sawn immediately after felling and converted to the sizes most desirable, depending upon the actual size of the trunk itself. Great care should be taken in stacking and the selection of stickers made, bearing in mind the fact that this timber is easily stained. It is advisable to use stickers of hardwood, preferably of a pale colour. Perfect stacking is necessary and great care should be taken to cover the top of the stack to prevent discoloration from moisture and other matter. For preference, the stack should be sited away from the possibility of driving rain and wind.

Birch

The birch which might be available to the home woodturner is likely to be of fairly slender girth and, for preference, it should be felled in March or April. The bark must be removed immediately after felling. The stickers should be fairly thick, up to 1½ in. (38 mm), and should be positioned vertically with good weighting on the top of the stack. One should aim at a fairly quick drying of the timber in the summer months.

Boxwood

Boxwood is a most peculiar timber and can rarely be obtained in large sizes. It should be converted fairly quickly but dried very slowly, otherwise it will develop very fine surface cracks which can ruin the appearance of the timber, although not seriously weaken it. Patience is perhaps the thing needed most with box, and careful, slow air drying is the best solution. It is recorded that the boxwood used by the engraver was invariably kept in boxes of sawdust and the sawdust was repeatedly changed as it absorbed the moisture from the boxwood. Certainly, it must have kept the wood in extremely good condition, bearing in mind that the grain would be running vertically through the blocks.

Timbers injurious to health

There are a number of timbers which can be injurious to health. The turner, both at work and in the home, would be well advised not to use any of these suspected timbers. The following list is by no means exhaustive; the turner should refer to an authority if he has any doubts.

Khaya anthothica and Khaya macherium

The former can be mistaken for mahogany and the latter is a substitute for rosewood. Both of these timbers are stated to be highly dangerous.

Makore, guarea, rosewood, teak, and iroko

These timbers can be harmful to people with allergic tendencies.

Mansonia and lapacho

Both of these woods have been found to cause dermatitis. They can also bring about irritation of the mucous membrane of the nose, with a possible effect on the ear canals which control balance. Many Education Authorities condemn the use of mansonia in schools.

Selection of timber

Careful examination of timber when selecting it for turning is essential. As mentioned earlier in the book, *never* use timber with cracks or splits, loose knots or flaws, beetle holes or deep resin ducts.

If timber with a high moisture content is used, it must first of all be rough turned, then left to dry before final turning to exact shape and size, otherwise the bowl may split in drying or its shape distort.

Reclaimed timber should be carefully examined for flaws, nails and small holes.

Timber from converted timbers of the hedgerow must be examined for wire staples, bolts and lead shot.

Measurement of timber

The UK and many other countries have changed from the imperial to the metric system of measurement (known as the SI system), so that the metre (m) has now become the unit of length, subdivided by the millimetre (mm)—m and mm are used as both singular and plural symbols. The square metre (m²) is the basic unit of area, and the cubic metre (m³) is the basic unit of volume.

Hardwood is available in lengths from 1.8 m rising by 100 mm increments; in widths from 150 mm rising by 10 mm increments or 25 mm increments; in thicknesses, 19, 25, 32, 38, 50, 63, 75, 100, and 125 mm, and thereafter by 25 mm increments. All thicknesses are basic and are cut sufficiently full to hold up to size in a seasoned condition.

Two conversion tables useful for the woodworker are given here.

Imperial inches	Metric millimetres	Described as	Metric millimetres	Imperial inches	Described as
1/32	.8	1 mm bare	1	.039	1/16 in. bare
1/16	1.6	1½ mm	2	.078	1/16 in. full
1/8	3.2	3 mm full	3	.118	1/8 in. bare
3/16	4.8	5 mm bare	4	.157	5/32 in.
1/4	6.4	6½ mm	5	.196	3/16 in. full
5/16	7.9	8 mm bare	6	.236	1/4 in. bare
3/8	9.5	9½ mm	7	.275	1/4 in. full
7/16	11.1	11 mm full	8	.314	5/16 in.
1/2	12.7	12½ mm full	9	.354	3/8 in. bare
9/16	14.3	14½ mm bare	10	.393	3/8 in. full
5/8	15.9	16 mm bare	20	.787	13/16 in. bare
11/16	17.5	17½ mm	30	1.181	13/16 in.
3/4	19.1	19 mm full	40	1.574	19/16 in. full
13/16	20.6	20½ mm	50	1.968	115/16 in. full
7/8	22.2	22 mm full	60	2.362	23/8 in. bare
15/16	23.8	24 mm bare	70	2.755	23/4 in.
1	25.4	25½ mm	80	3.148	31/8 in. full
2	50.8	51 mm bare	90	3.542	39/16 in. bare
3	76.2	76 mm full	100	3.930	315/16 in.
4	101.4	101½ mm	150	5.904	515/16 in. bare
5	127.0	127 mm	200	7.872	77/8 in.
6	152.4	152½ mm	300	11.808	1113/16 in.
7	177.5	178 mm bare	400	15.744	153/4 in.
8	203.2	203 mm full	500	19.680	1911/16 in.
9	228.6	228½ mm	600	23.616	235/8 in. bare
10	254.0	254 mm	700	27.552	279/16 in.
11	279.5	297½ mm	800	31.488	311/2 in.
12	304.8	305 mm bare	900	35.424	357/16 in.
18	457.2	457 mm full	1,000	39.360	393/8 in. bare
24	609.6	609½ mm			
36	914.4	914½ mm			

Converting square feet to square metres (rounded off to 3 decimal places)

square feet	square metres									
	0	1	2	3	4	5	6	7	8	9
0	—	0.093	0.186	0.279	0.372	0.464	0.557	0.650	0.743	0.836
10	0.929	1.022	1.115	1.203	1.301	1.394	1.486	1.579	1.672	1.765
20	1.858	1.951	2.044	2.137	2.230	2.323	2.415	2.508	2.601	2.694
30	2.787	2.880	2.973	3.066	3.159	3.252	3.345	3.437	3.530	3.623
40	3.716	3.809	3.902	3.995	4.088	4.181	4.274	4.366	4.459	4.552
50	4.645	4.738	4.831	4.924	5.017	5.110	5.203	5.295	5.388	5.481
60	5.574	5.667	5.760	5.853	5.946	6.039	6.132	6.224	6.317	6.410
70	6.503	6.596	6.689	6.785	6.875	6.968	7.061	7.154	7.246	7.339
80	7.432	7.525	7.618	7.711	7.804	7.897	7.990	8.083	8.175	8.268
90	8.361	8.454	8.547	8.640	8.733	8.826	8.919	9.012	9.104	9.197

Note: 1ft² equals 0.09290304m² exactly.

8 Preparation of Timber to be Turned on the Lathe

Mounting wood on the lathe

Mounting timber between centres

Starting with square-section material, draw diagonals on both ends and scribe a circle with a pair of compasses. Plane off the corners, then make saw cuts at one end, approximately ⅛ in. (3.2 mm) apart, to receive the lathe driving fork.

The timber can now be mounted on the lathe. Many turners fail to prepare timber in this way, but for beginners it is essential. Unprepared timber revolving on the lathe throws off large splinters from the corners, which can be dangerous. As the gouge cuts these corners, the timber tends to push the gouge back against the user which can be rather frightening. At the same time, the noise of the corners hitting the gouge can have a similar effect.

Fig. 8.1
For spindle work when mounting between centres

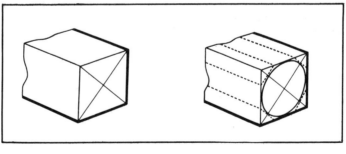

Fig. 8.2
Corners planed off

Fig. 8.3
Saw cuts

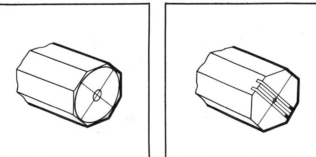

Timber mounted on the faceplate

Blocks of wood should, at the very least, have their corners removed. Draw diagonals to mark the centre, draw a circle with a pair of compasses or dividers. Saw off the corners. Ideally, if a bandsaw is available, saw out the complete disc.

Carefully centralize the faceplate, and use a bradawl to prepare the screw holes.

Timber held in the collar chuck

Select a piece of timber of a size appropriate to the particular job. It must be at least 2½ in. (63 mm) square to ensure that sufficient timber is available to be gripped by the collar.

Mount between centres, turn down the timber to 2 in. (50 mm) diameter, leaving a flange at one end of a size equal to the internal diameter of the chuck collar. When mounting the timber, hang the collar over the tailstock ready for testing the diameter as it is reduced. The testing should be done with the lathe stationary.

Remove the timber from the lathe, slide the collar over the end and screw up tightly.

Fig. 8.4
Sawing complete disc

Fig. 8.5
For bowl and box work

Fig. 8.6
For box and vase work when mounting to a collar chuck (1)

Fig. 8.7
For box and vase work when mounting to a collar chuck (2)

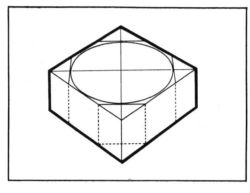
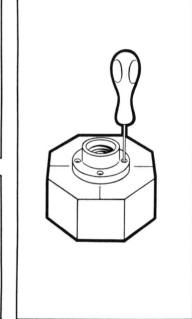
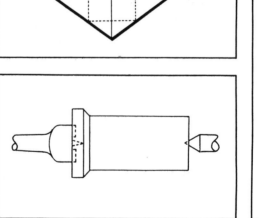
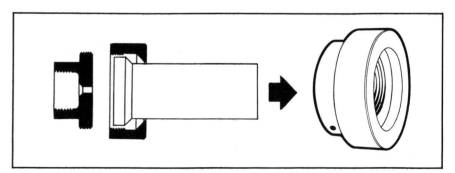

Attachments for mounting wood on the lathe

Collar chucks
   Chucks for egg-cups, serviette rings, boxes, and vases.

Cup chucks
   Chucks for holding timber for serviette rings, egg-cups, small boxes, and rings.

Faceplates
   Discs for large bowls, large boxes and larger work, such as standard lamp bases.

Glue chucks
   Chucks for attaching small discs for lids, small dishes, trays, and costume jewellery.

Screw-flange chucks
   Small discs for plates, mirror and picture frames, and small dishes.

Wood chucks
   Chucks for holding partly turned dishes, plates, and frames.

9 Lathe Turning and Boring Speeds

Speeds for turning

The speed of the lathe should be related to the size of timber being turned but very slow speeds can be dangerous, particularly if the lathe should slow down when the cutting tool is applied. Slower speeds will obviously tend to slow down progress, but this may also produce poor surfaces. The hardness or softness of the timber, its grain formation and whether it has an oil or resin content, must also have a bearing on the speed.

Turning speeds

Dia.	r.p.m.
1 in.	2850
2 in.	2400
3 in.	1500
4 in.	1000
6−8 in.	850
10−12 in.	700

A speed equal to the r.p.m. of the motor, i.e. 1425, will be found most suitable for the majority of jobs mounted between centres. Bowl and box work of over 4 in. diameter will need slower speeds and the user can best judge the optimum speed by trial. Excessive vibration of the machine must be avoided.

Lathes are generally fitted with three- or four-step pulleys as an integral part of the headstock; the motor pulley is a similar pulley but in reverse. Horsepower will be related to the height of centres of the machine. A fair guide is as follows:

6 in. centres	1 h.p.
5 in. centres	¾ h.p.
4½ in. centres	½ h.p.
4 in. centres	⅓ h.p.

Speeds for boring

Lathe speeds will depend on the type of boring tool being used and its size; a general rule is—fast speeds for small diameters, reducing as the hole sizes increase.

Boring speeds

Tool	Size (in.)	Speed (r.p.m.)
Flatbits (Ridgway R355)	All sizes	2500
Lamp standard auger (Ridgway R219)	$^{1}/_{4}$, $^{5}/_{16}$, $^{3}/_{8}$ (6, 8, 9.5 mm)	900
Wood drills (Ridgway R527)	$^{1}/_{8}$ to $^{1}/_{4}$ (3 to 6 mm)	2500
Lip and spur drills (Ridgway R509)	$^{1}/_{4}$ to $^{1}/_{2}$ (6 to 13 mm)	1500
Sawtooth cutters (Ridgway R542)	$^{3}/_{8}$ (9.5 mm)	1000
	$^{1}/_{2}$ (13 mm)	750
	$^{3}/_{4}$ (19 mm)	500
	1 (25 mm)	400
	$1^{1}/_{2}$ (38 mm)	250
	2 (50 mm)	200

It may not be possible to run the lathe at these exact speeds, and the turner may by experiment arrive at different figures to suit his lathe.

10 Finishing Woodturnings

Choice of finishes

When the design of a turning is being considered, the type of finish must also be discussed. The turner must ask himself the following questions before making a decision:

(1) Does the timber require treatment to improve the grain or colour?
(2) Will the finished work need protection against dirt, moisture, oil or grease?
(3) If the turning is a thin one or the grain very open, will the wood need to be sealed?
(4) Should the surface be glossy, satin or matt?
(5) Will the article require treatment to protect against contamination of food or by food?
(6) In use, will the article need cleaning from time to time?
(7) Will the article be used to contain hot food or drink?

Certainly, the choice of available finishes is wide enough to meet any of these requirements, but before polish is applied the surface of the timber must be smooth and as far as possible free from flaws. No polish will cover up the faults in a badly finished job; mostly, it will only accentuate them.

Wet finishes, like french polish, can be applied with pads made of soft cloth filled with cotton wool, and wax polishes with a soft cloth. Cellulose is best brushed on with a good-quality fine-bristle brush. Shavings, coarse cloth or hessian can be used for burnishing.

All polishes should be applied with the lathe stopped, but cutting back with steel wool or wet and dry paper is best carried out with the lathe running. Always burnish with the lathe running, constantly moving the burnishing material to avoid burning.

Abrasives

A wide variety of abrasive paper is available, the most common being:

Glasspaper. This consists of crushed glass glued to thick paper.

Garnet. This consists of powdered garnet stones, much harder than glass, glued to thick paper or linen cloth.

Aluminium oxide. This is an artificial abrasive, most commonly found in use in industry. It keeps sharp and does not clog quite so easily as glasspaper.

Silicon carbide. This is also an artificial abrasive glued to a waterproof paper. The finer grades are superb for cutting back polishes.

Abrasive papers are usually available in sheets 11 × 9 in. (280 × 229 mm).

Types of finish and details

Finish	Varieties available	Ease of application	Types of work for which suitable	Results to be expected	Advantages/ disadvantages
French polish	Button, orange, standard, white, etc.	Easy to brush on. Rubber work needs practice and care. Easy to finish 'satin' using wax	Best for spindle turnings, small work, table lamps, handle holders, napkin rings, etc.	For sheer quality of finish, the best. A soft sheen with wood shown at its best.	Not resistant to solvents, etc. Needs time, care and patience to apply
Cellulose	Brush or spray, matt, satin, gloss, etc.	Easy to apply by brush or spray (bulb or car foot pump). Can be burnished to a high gloss	Utility jobs where high resistance is not needed, e.g. tool handles	A 'surface' finish often high gloss. Adds little to quality of wood. Can look gluey	Can be brittle and none too permanent
Polyurethane	One- or two-pack (i.e. lacquer and curing agent). PU french polish (matt, satin or gloss)	Easy to apply by brush, pad or spray. Beware of having it too thick	Most types of turned work	Good results are obtained; gloss, satin or matt	Rather slow drying (except for two-pack types) and care needed in rubbing down between coats
Acid catalyst lacquer	Two-part lacquers	Floated on by brush. Can be rubbed on. Can be burnished or rubbed down with wire wool and wax	High resistance to solvents, hot water and alcohol	Good results if applied sparingly and rubbed down	Short 'pot' life. The only truly 'water-white' finish
Wax	Home-made. 85% beeswax, 15% carnauba. Proprietary (e.g. Johnson's, Nicholson's chilled, Briwax)	Very easy to apply over a sealer coat of french polish or other finish or to raw wood	Any piece of work not likely to be handled. Best for decorative pieces rather than utility	A lovely soft warm sheen	Finger and other marks show easily
Linseed oil, tung oil	Boiled or raw (terebine and gold size may be added)	Rubbed in with a rag	Anything except food containers	An excellent finish	Takes a very long time to reach a full oil finish. One application per day for several weeks
Teak oil	The original from Scandinavia. Others now available	Rubbed in with a rag	Any type of work at all	An excellent finish	Best on teak, afrormosia, etc., but can be used on any timber
Vegetable oil	Any cooking (corn) oil	Rubbed in with a rag	Salad bowls and all kinds of food containers	Gives a soft sheen	Will not turn rancid
Danish oil (Watco)	Clear, matt and gloss	Easy to apply—pad or brush. Can be rubbed down with wire wool, etc.	General use	Excellent finish: matt or gloss	Very resistant to wear

Abrasives for polishing

Silicon carbide wet and dry paper, particularly in the finer grades, is used for polishing. Steel wool, in grades 3, 2, 1, 0, 00, and 000, may also be used for cutting polishes.

Grading of abrasives

	Glasspaper	Garnet paper	Manufactured grits: aluminium oxide silicon carbide
			600
			500
			400
Extra fine			360
			320
		8/0	280
		7/0	240
	00 (flour)	6/0	220
		5/0	180
Fine	0	4/0	150
	1	3/0	120
	1½	2/0	100
	F2	1/0	80
Medium	M2	1/2	60
	S2	1	50
Coarse	2½	1½	40
	3	2	36
			30
			24
Very			20
coarse			16
			12

Use of abrasive papers

The use of abrasive papers on the lathe should be kept to a minimum. Use only fine grades of glasspaper, the coarser grades will only serve to deeply score the timber and make unnecessary work. The woodturner would be advised to use garnet paper as opposed to glasspaper, since garnet paper will not only retain its sharpness longer but the dust can easily be removed by shaking the paper. The aluminium oxide type of papers, in the finer grades, will give even longer service but they are often more difficult to obtain.

Techniques for glasspapering should be very carefully followed. First, remove the tee-rest and any other obstruction from the lathe bed. Secondly, the glasspaper must be held in the right hand, which is supported by the left hand. When working between centres, glasspapering must be carried out with the glasspaper underneath the work. Should the work snatch the paper from the hand, the glasspaper will move away from the operator without damage. Never place the hands on the top of the work, particularly the left hand, since the operator's attention may wander and the possibility of his little finger becoming engaged with the driving fork could have disastrous results.

The glasspapering of boxes and bowls must be carried out using the same precautions. In this case, hold the glasspaper in the right hand and support it with the left. Papering should take place with the paper held in the lower part of the box, i.e. in the position between half past and quarter to on the clock. Again, should the paper be snatched from the hand, it will move away from the operator without causing any damage to the operator's fingers. Keep the glasspaper constantly on the move, since holding it too firmly in one place may result in the burning of the timber, in addition to the hand or fingers.

Glasspapering can also be carried out with the lathe at rest. Here, the glasspaper can be moved in the direction of the grain rather than across the grain and a much finer surface will result.

All work which has been glasspapered should finally be burnished with a handful of shavings, preferably the shavings taken off the work itself. In this way, a sheen will be added to the timber similar to the sheen given by the tool when rubbing the wood. It is also suggested that a pad of coarse hessian can follow the application of the shavings; this will remove any dust or particles and again assist the burnishing operation.

Treatment of flaws in turned timber

Occasionally, a turning may be almost complete when a small hole or flaw appears which cannot be eliminated by further turning. A stopper must now be brought into use.

A good solution is to mix some wood dust, of the exact colour of the turned piece, with Araldite or one of the many types of epoxy resin. Use the fast-setting type, thoroughly mix the glue and hardener together, then add the dust to saturation point. Push well into the flaw and leave a surplus for final papering down. This filling will polish well and the flaw will hardly be noticed.

Proprietary brands of stopping can be used but must be carefully selected.

Beaumontage, in sticks of many colours, must be applied with a warm knife. Alternatively, heat can be applied with a pencil-bit electric soldering iron, which is quick, clean and precise.

Brummer or Borden stopping, available in various colours, may be used but care must be taken to colour-match before applying. Take care to apply the stopping to the fault not to the surrounding timber, otherwise with open-grained timber the Brummer or Borden will act as a grain filler and make the area conspicuous.

The use of so-called plastic wood should be avoided.

Hand-scraping of turned work

The turner occasionally experiences great difficulty in obtaining a perfect surface from the cutting tool. The scraping chisel may provide the solution to this problem, but even so some timbers, particularly tropical ones, may still stubbornly refuse to finish cleanly. The turner must now resort to hand-scraping, with the machine stopped, in order to tackle the offending area.

Old machine hacksaw blades make ideal scrapers. They can be ground to shape on the grinder, giving a bevel similar to the lathe scrapers, and used in the ground state. Two suggested shapes are shown with their purpose indicated, but individuals will shape up to suit their own particular design problem.

Fig. 10.1
Hand-scrapers: left, scraping inside curves; right, scraping outside curves

To hand-scrape, stop the lathe and, if a headstock spindle lock is fitted, lock the work to prevent rotation. Wedge the spindle if a lock is not fitted.

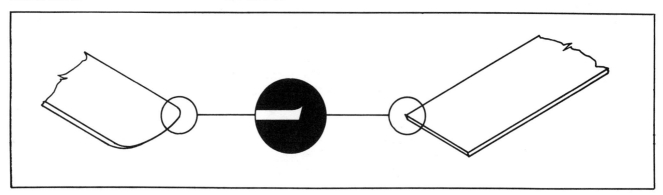

Scrape carefully, using the scraper in a similar way to the bench scraper. It can be moved in any direction to cut back the offending rough patch.

11 The Tools in Use

Holding the tools

There has always been some difference of opinion about the way to hold tools. The basic rule is that the tools should be held firmly but lightly, never rigidly so that flexibility is lost. Many pupils when they first begin to turn cling to the tools, giving the impression that these are a lifeline between themselves and disaster; their knuckles turn white and their faces ashen. This is largely due to the preachings of many so-called experts who talk about 'dig-ins', flying timbers, fingerless hands and the like. Complete relaxation should be the watchword—start your turning education by working between centres and following instructions; test drive if you like by trying out each cut, turning the lathe by hand (get someone to assist here).

Choose your tools carefully, preferably those with handles designed to fit the hand comfortably. Many handles are too large and clumsy; they should be waisted towards the end to receive the hand without the possibility of the hand running off. Obviously, there must be enough wood to give strength, but very heavy handles destroy flexibility in the turner's hand. It must be remembered that these tools are used by children and women whose hands tend to be smaller than those of the average man.

Fig. 11.1
Woodturning tool handle

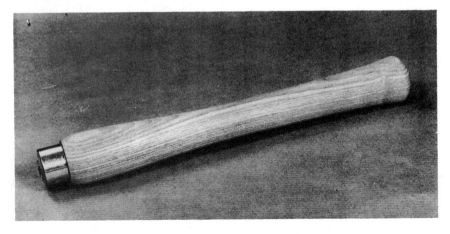

Hold the handle lightly at its extremity with the right hand, with the four fingers of the left hand wrapped over the top of the chisel or gouge and the thumb underneath. Shavings are deflected away from the turner and the cutting action tends to be dampened by this hold.

Fig. 11.2
Holding the tool—hands at the extremities

There are, however, several occasions when this grip masks out the work. The hold must, in these cases, be changed to one of the thumb on top and the first finger underneath. This is particularly important when marking out, parting off or beading.

The thumb-on-top position when using the gouge has the great disadvantage of allowing the shavings to slide down the curve of the gouge, hit the thumb and fly into your face. The thumb-on-top grip has a further disadvantage in that the hand must be brought well down the blade in order to clear the tool rest.

There are few rules which need to be remembered in woodturning; once these are mastered the woodturner should have no difficulty in cutting timber correctly.

Fig. 11.3
Left-hand well up deflects the shavings

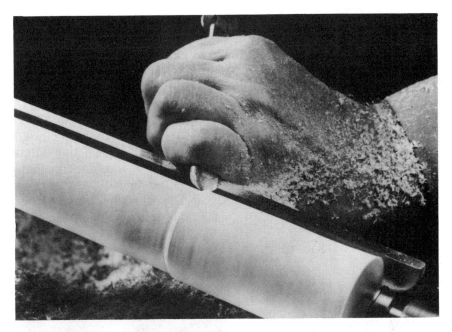

Fig. 11.4
Using the parting tool—thumb on top

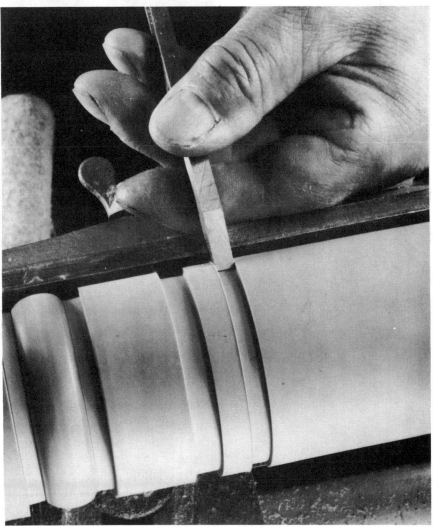

The basic rule with cutting tools is that the bevel of the tool should be looking at the wood; that is, the tool when placed on the wood must have its bevel rubbing the wood—in effect the timber will always be supporting the tool. None of the cutting tools should, in fact, cut when first brought into contact with the timber. Slope the chisel or gouge in the direction in which the tool is to move. This applies both to between-centres work and faceplate work.

The right hand should be holding the handle at its extremity firmly but lightly, and its function will be to raise the tool so that the cutting edge comes in contact with the turning wood. The amount the right hand is raised will dictate the thickness of the shaving. Once the amount of cut is arrived at, the tool is moved easily along the tee-rest for the total length of cut required, the same angle being maintained throughout. The gouge which is moved slowly along the wood when working between centres will produce a fairly flat and even surface once the timber has been cut to round.

Fig. 11.5
Tool slopes in the direction in which it is to move

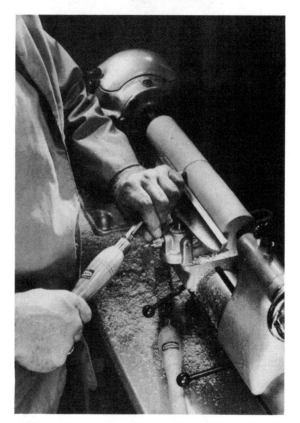

Cutting

Using the gouge—spindle turning

For roughing between centres, two different gouges—the shallow gouge and the deep gouge—can be used, but both are ground square across.

The shallow gouge, either of standard or long and strong type, will produce a wide fairly thin shaving, while the deep standard gouge, either ¾ in. (19 mm) or 1¼ in. (32 mm) across, will bring off thick rope-like shavings.

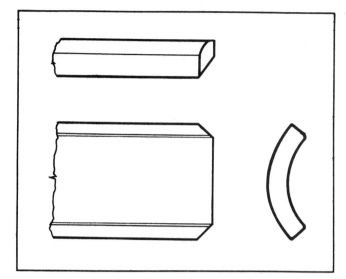

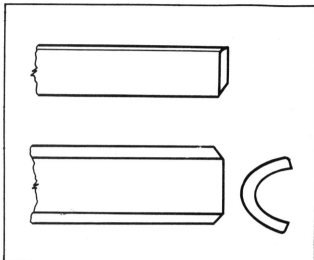

Fig. 11.6
Shallow gouge

Fig. 11.7
Deep standard gouge

The cutting action of these gouges is the same; the basic rule must be to let the bevel rub. Raising the right hand will produce a cut, and the amount the handle is raised determines the thickness of the cut.

Slope the gouge in the direction of movement along the wood, then lay it over on its side and the bevel will tend to direct the movement of the tool in the direction of its slope.

No force is required. Indeed, if the angle of slope is increased, the gouge will move to the left almost of its own volition.

With the deep gouge, any part of the cutting edge can be used. This gouge removes wood very rapidly, and when laid completely on its side it has a similar action to that of the chisel.

Using the chisel—spindle turning

The skew or ground square across 1 in. (25 mm) chisel is used for general planing. To achieve a perfectly flat surface, the chisel must be used. Remember once again the basic rule of cutting—the bevel of the tool must rub the wood. The bevel will rub only if the left-hand lower corner of the chisel is in contact with the tool rest; in fact, the chisel is twisted to arrive at this position. Thus, the tool is supported not only by being in contact with the tool rest, but also by its bevel resting on the wood. Should this position not be adopted, then one can expect trouble. For example, if we attempt to cut at C (see Fig. 11.11) moving towards the headstock, since the bevel cannot rub the work (rest on the wood if you like) the chisel will snatch at the corner and dig out a piece of the wood. This extreme end can only be planed by moving the chisel towards the tailstock; that is, turn the tool to face the other way so that the bevel rubs and the chisel rests firmly on the tool rest.

The chisel must also be held at an angle as illustrated; thus, only the centre or the lower portion between A and B will cut. The cut is brought about by raising the handle of the tool, and the thickness of shaving is controlled by the amount the hand is raised. Shavings should be flat and continuous, the cutting quite effortless and the finish perfect. The fact that the bevel rubs the wood immediately after the point of cut brings about the polish; thus, the finer the finish on the bevel of the chisel, the better the finish on the wood.

At no time must the top half of the chisel be used when planing the timber, otherwise serious harm can be done to the work. Care must also be taken not to cut with the extremity of the tool at B, otherwise there is a possibility of undercutting and tearing the timber.

If a taper is being cut, the action of cutting is the same; the turner working from the large diameter to the small—downhill, in fact.

The chisel is used in a similar way when rounding over the end of a cylinder, the only variation being that the handle of the tool must be moved around so that the cutting edge follows the curve and the bevel rubs.

Fig. 11.8
Skew chisel

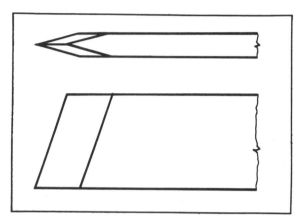

Fig. 11.9
Planing with the chisel

Fig. 11.10
Planing with the chisel

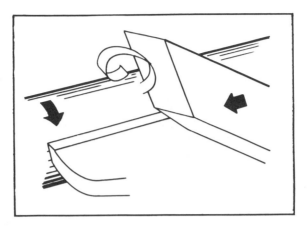

Fig. 11.11
Planing

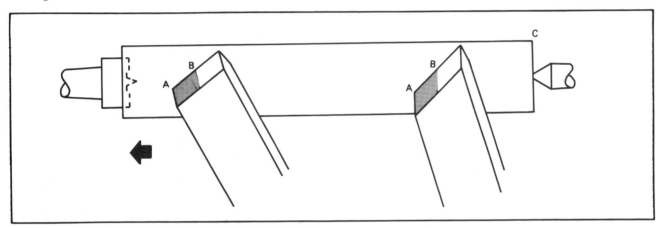

Fig. 11.12
Taper cutting

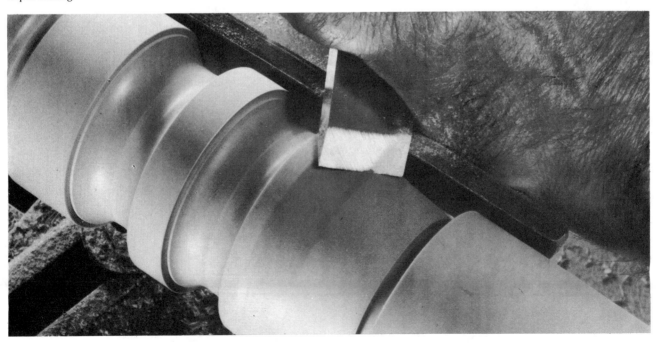

Fig. 11.13
Skew chisel—rounding over

Steadies

When planing very thin timber it will be necessary to support the work, otherwise vibration will be set up, the timber will tend to move away from the cutting tool, and a poor surface or a spiral-cut surface will result.

There are several steadies manufactured, but these are based on the metalworker's steady and tend to be cumbersome and unsatisfactory in use. The old woodworking craftsmen used one made of wood, having a weighted wedge keeping a notched arm in constant contact with the turned spindle.

Fig. 11.14
Wooden steady

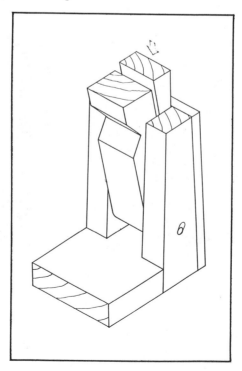

For many years the author has used a wheeled steady with a pair of spring-adjusted wheels always in contact with the timber.

Perhaps the best way is to use the fingers to support the work; only very light pressure is needed.

Fig. 11.15
Steady designed for the Myford lathe

Fig. 11.16
Using the fingers as a steady

Parting

When using the parting tool, the bevel still rubs the wood, the cut being brought on by raising the right hand. There is a slight tendency for the tool to move back against the user when the cut comes on. Hold the tool firmly but lightly and no difficulty will be experienced. Alternatively, the parting tool can be pushed straight into the work. Wherever possible, part slightly wider than the thickness of the parting tool itself in order to reduce rubbing and counteract the tendency of the chisel to overheat.

Fig. 11.17
Parting off or marking out

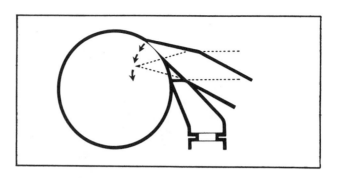

Beading

The same technique is needed as for rounding. Use a ¼ in. (6 mm) beading chisel, for this work; this is particularly important with small beads, since the larger chisel will prevent the use of the centre of the tool and also the rolling of the tool over the curve. Work from the centre, downhill, making the perfection of the curve with a quick twist of the wrist.

Fig. 11.18
Beading with a chisel

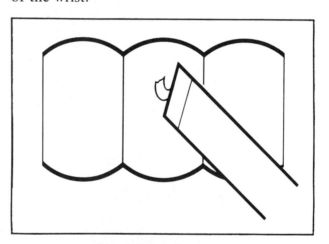

Fig. 11.19
Cutting a bead with the beading chisel

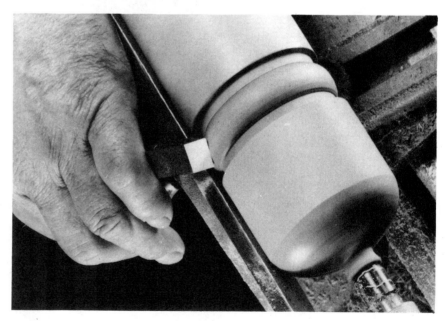

Squaring the ends or cutting shoulders

In this sort of cutting, the long corner of the tool is used. The bevel of the chisel must be squared with the line of centres, by moving the handle of the chisel to the left. This enables the bevel of the tool to rub the wood as it cuts. The best approach to this cut is to keep the handle of the skew chisel low, then raise it slowly to enable the long corner to gradually cut into the shoulder. The chisel can be pushed straight in but care must be exercised to avoid burning. It is extremely important not only to see that the chisel is sharp, but also to maintain a perfect long corner.

Fig. 11.20
Squaring the end using the long corner of the skew chisel

Decorative cuts—coving

These cuts can be made with the round-nose gouge, which is a shallow standard-size gouge having its nose shaped like the end of the little finger, or with a deep long and strong gouge with rounded nose.

As with every other cutting tool, the bevel of these gouges must rub the wood. To use them to cut coves, the cut must start with the gouge lying on its side; by twisting the tool with a wrist movement and at the same time bringing on the cut, the gouge can be pushed down the cove to complete the cut by finishing on its back. Separate cuts are made from each side of the cove to end in the centre; with the bevel rubbing, a smooth finish is assured.

Fig. 11.21
Standard gouge—round nose

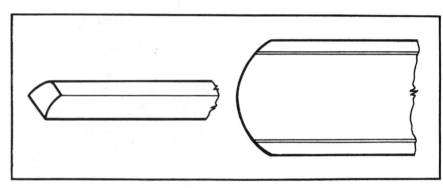

Fig. 11.22
Deep long and strong gouge—round nose

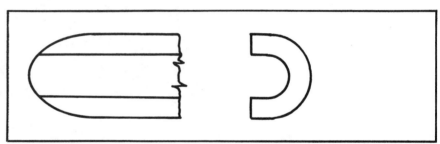

Fig. 11.23
Coving—using the gouge from the right

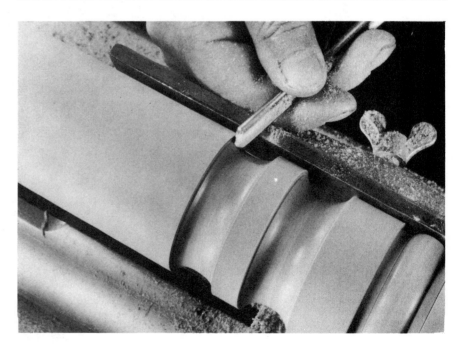

Fig. 11.24
Coving—using the gouge from the left

Fig. 11.24
Coving—using the gouge from the left

Fig. 11.25
Movement of the gouge

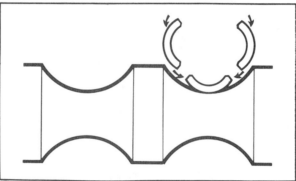

The beginner may have one slight problem with coving. With the gouge lying on its side, the moment the cut is brought on the gouge will tend to move rapidly to the left or right depending on which side the tool is lying. This can be most disconcerting and, of course, such a movement may destroy an adjacent finished section. To avoid this happening, it is best to make a small groove at each side of the cove in which to locate the gouge.

Off-centre turning

Many people imagine that only purely cylindrical work can be carved out on the lathe. This is a complete fallacy, since not only can a piece of wood be turned on a number of different centres but, in manufacture, lathes are designed with adjustable centres to make elliptical and other non-cylindrical work possible.

One of the most interesting and exciting jobs to turn using offsetting is the cabriole leg.

Prepare timber, mount between centres and mark out to leave a pummel at the headstock end. This pummel will later have mortices cut in it to receive the stool rails.

In addition, mark out two centres at the tailstock end, one true and another halfway between the true centre and the outer edge of the leg.

Turn down to round and turn a bead close to the foot end as in step 1 (illustrated).

Fig. 11.26
Cabriole leg: (1) turning to round—cutting the foot bead

Re-centre using the offset centre at the tailstock end, also slightly offset in the opposite direction at the driven end (step 2).

Fig. 11.27
Cabriole leg: (2) leg offset—cutting the taper

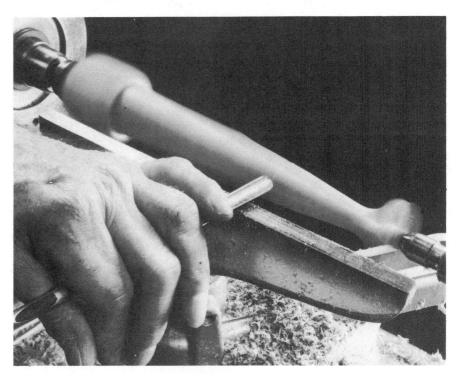

Set the lathe running and then, between the bead and the pummel, a taper form is seen. A sheet of white paper at the back of the lathe will aid vision. Use a round-nose gouge to curve into this apparent taper, curving away from the bead but not touching it.

The bevel rubs and the gouge moves down the curve into the straight (step 3). Glasspaper will probably have to be used to blend the true and off-centre turned curves together.

Fig. 11.28
Cabriole leg: (3) completing the bead—leg returned to centres

Now return the leg to its true centres and, using the chisel, round over the foot (step 4).

When turning the other three legs it will be necessary to use a cardboard template to ensure a perfectly matched set.

Fig. 11.29
Cabriole leg: (4) removing the waste prior to parting off

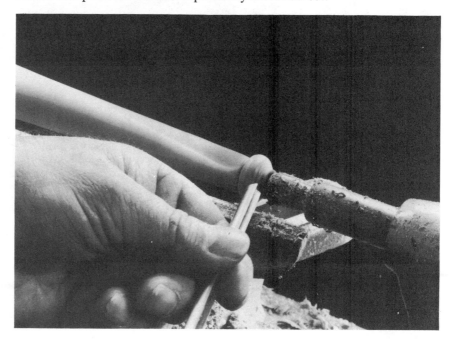

Faceplate turning

Easily the most popular and efficient tool for this work is the deep long and strong gouge—preferably the ⅜ in. (9.5 mm) size ground square across; the angle of grind is 40−45 deg.

Once again, to cut the wood in the way it likes to be cut the bevel of the tool must rub, but unlike the gouge in spindle work, where in the main the centre of the gouge is doing the cutting, the side of the gouge does the cutting while the centre of the bevel is rubbing and resting on the wood. Because of the thick section of the tool, a very strong cutting edge is presented to the work; thus, cutting becomes easy and no problems arise.

Before starting to use the gouge, check that the bowl block is securely screwed to a faceplate. Mount the work to the lathe and begin by tackling the outside shaping first. Move the gouge from the centre towards the outside. Let the bevel rub, keep the handle low and raise the tool to commence the cut. Move the tool round the curve to ensure that the bevel will always be bearing and the edge of the gouge cutting.

Fig. 11.30
Use of the gouge—outside turning of a bowl

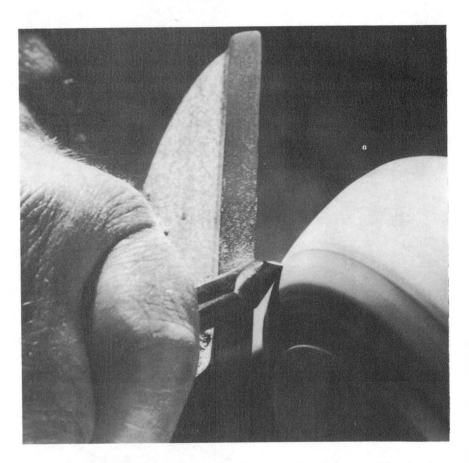

To cut the inside of the bowl, having completed the outside shaping, accurately re-centre. Use the parting tool to cut a groove to act as a starting point for the gouge. Make a hole in the centre of the bowl to remove that often troublesome bit and also to give an indication of depth. To cut the hole, a sawtooth cutter or flatbit can be used; watch the long brad point of the latter. An easier and quicker way is to use the round-nose standard gouge like a shell bit to do this, pressing the little finger hard against the wood to measure the depth.

Commence cutting from the point-of-start groove, place the gouge on its side, with the centre of the bevel rubbing, raise the handle slightly to put on the cut and sweep the tool easily into the middle of the bowl. The short bevel of the ⅜ in. (9.5 mm) long and strong gouge makes it possible for the tool to follow a quick curve and, at the same time, keep its centre rubbing.

Fig. 11.31
Movement of the gouge—turning the outside of a bowl on the left of the headstock

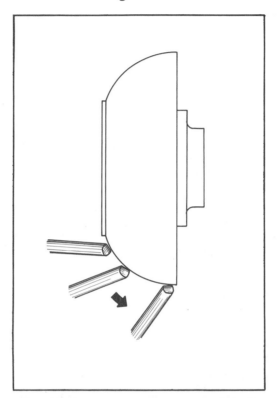

Fig. 11.32
Removing centre and indicating depth with the ¼ in. spindle gouge

The gouge *must* be moved from the outside to the centre and, while maintaining the same degree of cut, the handle must be moved in the vertical plane to enable the centre of the gouge to cut into the exact centre of the bowl. When cutting the outside of the bowl, the gouge handle should be kept as low as possible, the bevel should rub and, in this case, the right hand should move the gouge towards the user to put on the cut. Maintain the angle of the tool throughout the cut, keeping the handle as low as possible. Since the gouges are held on their sides, it is vitally necessary to start the cut from the small groove near the rim of the bowl.

It should be possible to remove the whole of the waste quite quickly; the last cut or two should be fining ones to ensure a clean smooth finish.

Fig. 11.33
Removing the waste with the ³/₈ in. deep long and strong gouge

Scraping

Scraping tools, used for either roughing or finishing, have a different cutting action. Scrapers are placed squarely on the tee-rest and therefore cannot have a slicing action; the right hand must be raised to a position higher than the tee-rest in order to allow the hooked cutting edge of the tool to scrape the wood.

A well-sharpened scraping tool will cut a shaving, but because the bevel cannot rub the wood it cannot at the same time burnish the wood. As a result, the finished surface fails to give that polished appearance so desirable for wood turned on the lathe. Timber scraped in this way must, in the end, have further finishing from abrasive paper before it is ready to accept burnishing with shavings and final polishing. Nevertheless, the scraper must be regarded as a finishing tool for faceplate work. Many people suggest that this is the only safe tool for beginners, particularly schoolchildren, to use. Frankly, anyone can use a scraper, but there is little or no satisfaction to be gained from its use. To see the ribbon shavings flying from a well-sharpened gouge or chisel is to have gained the ultimate in cutting satisfaction. The use of scrapers

Fig. 11.34
In scraping, the tool trails.

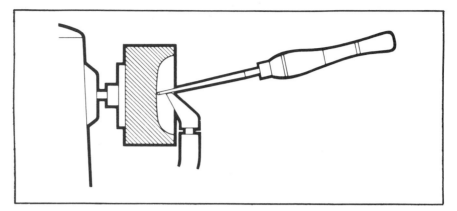

in spindle work is to be deplored, since nothing is safer than a chisel or gouge correctly applied; indeed, the scraper could be dangerous here.

In use, where the hook edge has been correctly formed, the scraper will remove clean shavings, without dust. Some users advocate an extremely heavy-bladed tool with an over-built handle, claiming the need for this by underlining the heaviness required in the cut and the need to damp down the vibration. This is quite unnecessary with the lightly *cutting* well-sharpened scraper.

Just as we scrape wood on the bench with a cabinet scraper, so we must apply the technique to the lathe. The cabinet scraper is sharpened with a hook and cuts by being angled to the hook, so that the hook can work. The scraper on the lathe must, therefore, lay flat on the tool rest, with the handle raised to allow it to 'trail'. The tool cuts slightly below centre.

General notes on cutting

The beginner would be well advised to make a dummy run with each tool before starting up the lathe, wherever possible rotating the lathe by hand and noting the cutting action which is likely to take place.

Wherever an error is made with a particular tool, the turner is also advised to reconstruct the fault. Stop the lathe and attempt to fit the tool exactly into the faulty cut—this is usually possible and will enable the turner to see his error and avoid repeating it.

If a great deal of weight or force is required to produce a cut, the tool is either not sharp or is being applied incorrectly.

Burning or discoloration of the cutting edge suggests that too much weight is being used or an edge needs attention.

Noise when cutting usually indicates a wrongly applied tool or one which is not sharp.

Remember, wood will 'sing' when being cut correctly, whereas any other noise indicates that for some reason the cutting is not being done properly.

Ribbing on lathe work

Many woodturners will, from time to time, experience the appearance of what looks like a rather coarse screw thread on the work, either in a spiralling effect on the face of a bowl or a thread effect on work between centres. This ribbing is usually caused by using badly sharpened tools, which tend to make cutting difficult. The turner will have to hold the tool too firmly and rigidly and push against the timber in order to obtain a cut. The timber reacts to this treatment and resists cutting, the tool tending to depress the softer growth and ride over the harder growth; this is particularly noticeable when there is a marked difference between spring and autumn growth. When working between centres, if the work is not securely held, in other words if the tailstock dead centre is not firmly home in the recess in the end of the work, this will also cause the timber to move away from the tool and a spiralling effect may be created in this way. This looseness of the working piece will also produce a similar result on the disc held on a faceplace.

Boring

Using the lamp standard shell auger

To bore safely using the shell auger, a boring attachment for the lathe is needed.

There are two types—the Graduate lathe attachment with a tailstock mandrel fitting, and the Graduate lathe attachment which replaces the tee-rest and tailstock.

Fig. 11.35
Long-hole boring attachment—tail-stock type

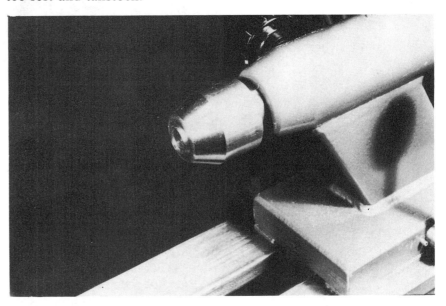

The timber is best turned between centres using the cup-type centre in the tailstock. This centre leaves a circular groove in the end of the timber which exactly matches the cup centre of the attachment. When the work has been polished, before removing it from the lathe, the flex hole will need to be bored.

When using the tee-rest inserted attachment, bring up the dead centre to locate the attachment exactly at centre height before tightening down on the locking screw.

Bring up the attachment and accurately place the timber in position, winding the cup centre part of the attachment tightly into the timber using the Allen key provided. With the timber securely held, tighten the locking screw by means of the Allen key.

Fig. 11.36
Long-hole boring attachment—the Ridgway lamp standard auger

To bore the hole, pass the auger through the tailstock and into the attachment. Switch on the lathe and push the auger into the revolving timber. Remove the auger several times to eject the chips from the shell of the auger. Bore the hole to within ½ in. (13 mm) of the headstock end. Part off the work and assemble to the base.

Alternatively, bore halfway along the length, remove the driving fork and substitute a counterbore centre to drive the workpiece; then reverse and bore through from the opposite end—the holes will meet.

Great care should be taken to avoid damage to the nose of the tool, particularly by running the auger through the wood into the lathe fork centre.

Fig. 11.37
Long-hole boring using the dead centre to check height and line of the boring attachment

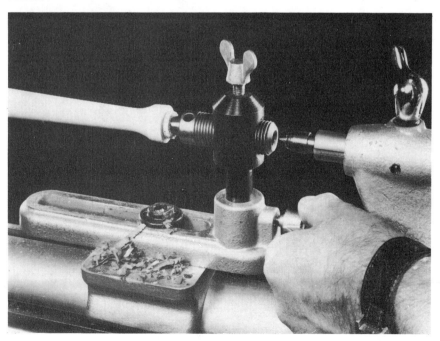

Care should also be taken when inserting the auger into and through the long-hole boring attachment of the lathe, to avoid damage to the cutting edges.

Frequently, withdraw the auger to tip out the waste, otherwise a solid bullet of waste will form in the shell to prevent the auger cutting and eventually burn and draw the temper at the cutting end.

Using the flatbit

This tool is useful for boring in all timbers. A fast speed is indicated in the table on page 73, and this must be carefully observed.

Fit the bit into the tailstock chuck, making sure that the jaws register on the flats of the bit. Tighten down firmly.

Bring the bit up to the work, secure the tailstock and rotate the work by hand to allow the brad point of the bit to register the centre of the work. Start up the lathe and wind the flatbit into the wood. Care must be taken not to feed the bit too quickly, otherwise it may tend to follow the softer grain and run off-centre. Having bored to the required depth, stop the lathe before withdrawing the bit. Take care, when measuring the depth of the hole, to allow for the length of the brad point.

Fig. 11.38
Serviette rings—boring out with the flatbit

Using the sawtooth machine bit

This cutter is superior to any other for boring holes in end grain on the lathe. It will be found most suitable for boring boxes, rings, serviette rings, salt and pepper mills and similar work. It bores a clean smooth hole in all timbers.

Assemble the cutter in the tailstock drill chuck and tighten the chuck firmly. The escapements of the cutter should be placed in such a position as to permit the easy passage of chips out of the work—this generally means at a quarter to and quarter past 'clock' position. Set the lathe to run at the speed suggested in the table on page 73. Bring up the tailstock, tighten down on its locking lever and, with the lathe stationary, wind the drill forward until the brad point of the cutter contacts the timber; then rotate the lathe by hand to score the centre. Start the lathe, wind the cutter into the revolving timber; the speed of feed should be as fast as the lathe will allow without slowing down. A fast rate of feed is essential, otherwise dust falling between the inside of the hole and the periphery of the bit may heat up and scorch. A slow feed will possibly burn the bit.

The speed of the machine must be related to the size of the hole being bored: small holes, fast speed; large holes, slower speed.

Fig. 11.39
Boring a box with the sawtooth machine cutter

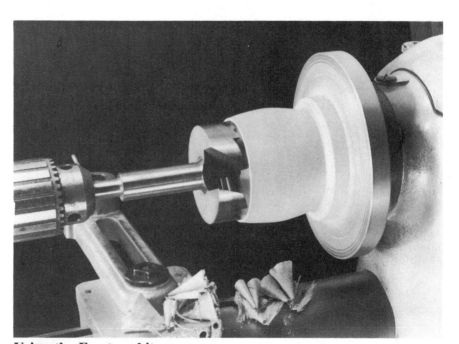

Using the Forstner bit

Machine speed with this bit should again be regulated according to the size of the hole: small holes, fast speed; large holes, slower speed. Rate of feed must be fairly fast, otherwise the rim of the tool may be burnt.

The bit can be used on the lathe in exactly the same way as the sawtooth cutter, but is only suitable for boring shallow holes. Particular attention must be paid to the rate of feed, as with the sawtooth cutter.

12 Turning Techniques Applied

Handles for woodturning tools

Tools for woodturning are generally available both handled and un-handled. The professional turner prefers, in most cases, to make his own handles to suit the tools, his hand and his particular methods.

Certainly, the first requirement is that the handle should be designed to fit the hand but at the same time it must be strong enough to hold the blade securely and resist vibration by the work. Many professionals use tools with very long handles which use the body for support.

Fig. 12.1
A *Woodturning tool handle in ash*

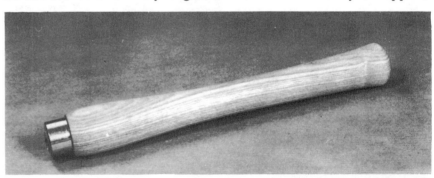

B *Turning tool handle*

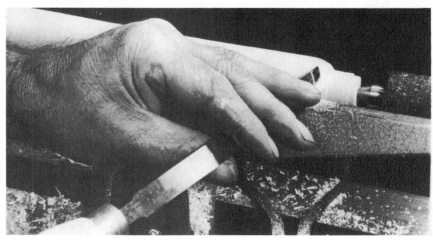

C *Turning tool handle—shaping with the chisel*

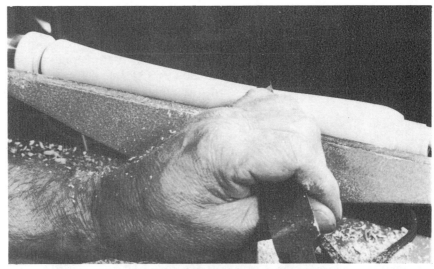

D *Turning tool handle—fitting the ferrule*

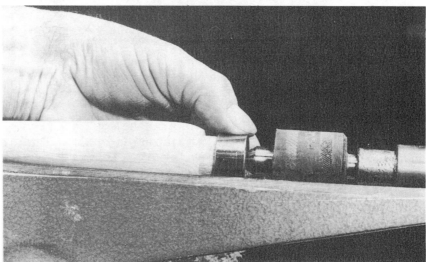

E *Turning tool handle—boring the hole for the tang*

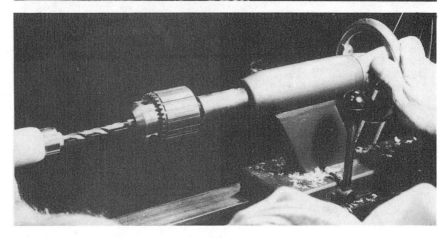

The handle design shown can be sized up or down to suit the type of tool—long and strong, standard, or smaller homeworker size tool. The sizes can be varied to suit the individual, but the shape will be found adequate to give comfort to the hand and receive the tang of the blade without lack of strength at the ferrule end.

Ash or beech should be used for handles and brass for the ferrules, but any good quality hardwood may be pressed into use.

Prepare the timber and mount between centres. Select a suitable ferrule and, if possible, place this over the tailstock centre so that it may be used to measure the turning of the ferrule end and finally be slipped into place when the turning is complete.

Rough down with the gouge and plane with a chisel to the finished size. Use the parting tool to size down the ferrule end, checking with the actual ferrule. Push the ferrule into position. Polish the handle and finally part off.

It is possible to bore the hole to receive the tang by placing a drill chuck in the tailstock and using a wood drill of correct size. Bring the tailstock up, so that the point of the drill is exactly located in the dead centre hole, and lock down. Lightly support the handle by the left hand, switch on the lathe and carefully move the drill into the handle by turning the tailstock wheel. After reaching the required depth, switch off the machine before withdrawing the drill.

Turning a long-hole boring auger handle

Prepare a piece of timber for turning between centres; ash or beech would be entirely suitable.

Mount between centres and use a roughing gouge to turn down to round.

Mark out the length and detail of the handle using a pencil.

Use the parting tool to cut grooves to mark the length limits.

With a 1 in. (25 mm) skew chisel, plane the wood to size and shape. When shaping, work downhill; that is, from large to small diameter.

Part down to within ¼ in. (6 mm) of centre. Use the skew chisel to roll over the ends. Remove rest, burnish with shavings and polish.

Replace rest and part off.

Mark the centre of the handle and bore a hole to receive a length of dowel rod which will, when assembled to the auger, prevent possible rotation of the tool itself when boring on the lathe.

Fig. 12.2
A *Handle for a Ridgway long-hole boring auger*

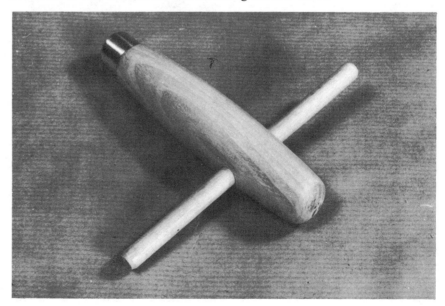

B *Handle for Ridgway long-hole boring auger*

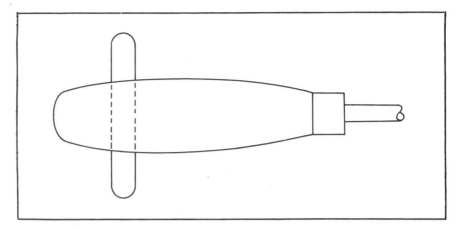

Turning a bowl

Prepare the timber for mounting to a faceplate or Universal chuck ring. Screw the work to the headstock mandrel, and bring up the rest as close to the work as possible. Select a roughing gouge which can be of the ground-square-across variety, shallow or deep-fluted.

Fig. 12.3
A *Shallow bowl*

B *Disc mounted to six-in-one chuck using chuck ring (deep long and strong gouge used)*

Turn down to round; let the bevel rub, bringing on the cut by raising the hand.

Change the rest so that it lies close to the wood and across the width of the bowl, so that the outside of the bowl can be cut, working from the centre to the outer edge.

Remember that the bowl will need to be re-chucked to permit the inside to be turned. Either cut a recess to locate a faceplate or a dovetail recess to receive the six-in-one Universal chuck. This will ensure perfect centricity upon reversal. Use the faceplate or chuck to check the fit.

C *Turning to round*

D *Cutting chuck recess*

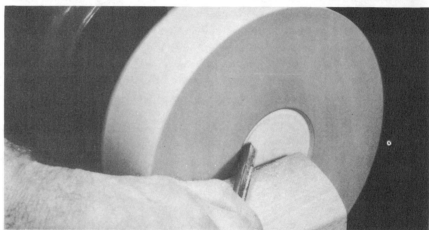

E *Cutting the dovetail corner with the skew chisel*

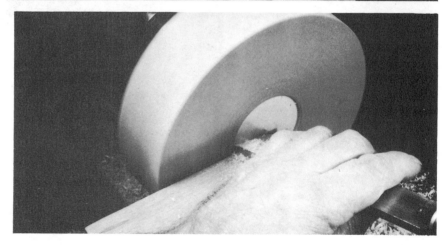

Keep the handle of the long and strong ⅜ in. (9.5 mm) deep gouge well down, let the bevel rub and move the tool around the curve from the centre to the outside, but let the first cut start close to the edge and work back towards the centre at each successive cut. Fairly coarse shavings can be taken at first, but when arriving at the correct shape, final cuts can be light. With the bevel rubbing and a polished bevel on the tool, a fairly smooth finish will result.

Should parts of the end grain be rough, stop the lathe and scrape by hand.

F *Shaping the outside with the gouge*

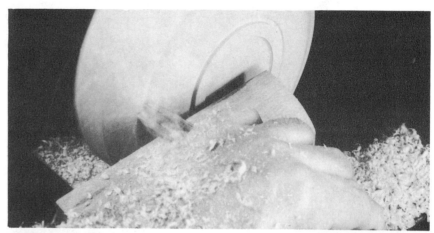

G *Shaping (i)*

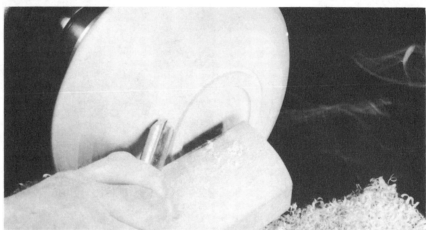

H *Shaping (ii)*

Some timbers may require the use of scraping chisels. Remember to let the tool trail, and take light finishing cuts.

Polish the outside.

Remove the job from the lathe, unscrew the plate, reassemble the faceplate or chuck and place back on the lathe. Place the rest across the face of the bowl.

Use the parting tool to mark the inside diameter of the bowl. This groove will also act as a point of start for the gouge.

J *Outside turning complete*

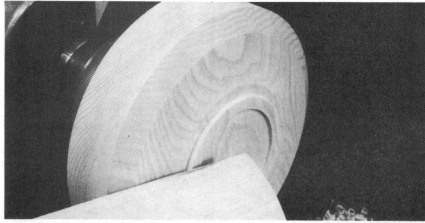

K *Polishing*

L *Bowl reversed—marking a point of start with the parting tool*

Remove the centre of the bowl to give an indication of final depth. Use a flatbit or sawtooth cutter mounted in the tailstock chuck. Alternatively, the ¼ in. (6 mm) round-nose gouge can be used—this will cut in the same way as a shell bit. The little finger of the left hand rubbing the wood can be used to gauge the depth.

Take the ⅜ in. (9.5 mm) long and strong deep gouge and commence with the tool on its side, handle well down, centre of bevel rubbing at the groove. The point of start will instantly locate the tool and prevent its inclination to move towards the outside edge.

M *Removing the centre with the ¼ in. round-nose gouge*

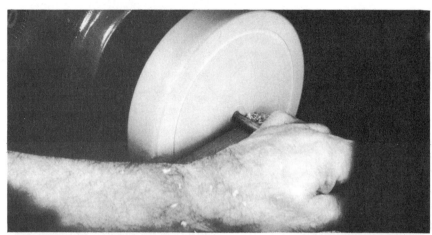

N *Marking out completed*

O *Shaping with the ⅜ in. long and strong gouge*

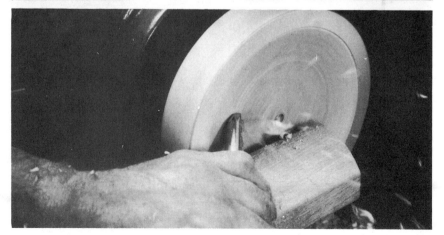

Raise the right hand to put on the cut. Move the gouge towards the centre and, at the same time, raise the handle so that the gouge scribes an arc over the face to make its centre meet the centre of the bowl. Should this not take place, the gouge will go across the face above the bowl centre, leaving it uncut.

Return to make each cut from the point of start.

Fairly coarse shavings, without great effort, will quickly remove the centre and final smoothing cuts can be taken with the same tool re-sharpened.

Finish the inside of the bowl as necessary. Polish and remove from the lathe.

The recess can be filled with a disc of cork to hide the screw holes, but if the Universal chuck is used, this will not be needed.

P *Shaping (iii)*

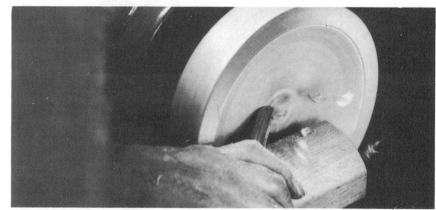

Q *Shaping (iv)*

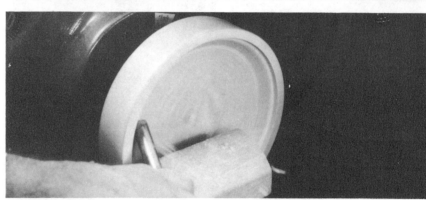

R *Finishing with fine paper*

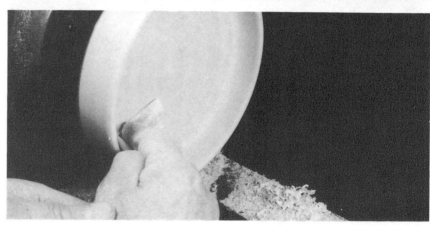

S *Polishing with a hessian pad*

Turning a box

It is envisaged that the box design will incorporate a knob and lid, with the lid fitting into the internal diameter of the box. Having designed the box, select a suitable piece of timber and check v⸱ry carefully to see that it is free from cracks or surface checks of any kind. Having first of all removed the corners, mount the piece of wood on a small faceplate.

Fig. 12.4
A *Box in ash*

B *Material screwed to faceplate*

Place the faceplate on the lathe, and bring the tailstock up into position so that the piece of wood may be turned round, as in normal spindle turning.

When down to round but not necessarily to the exact outside diameter, first mark out with a pencil, then take a fine parting tool or use the point of a chisel to mark out the limits of the lid, the knob and the box itself.

C *Roughing to size*

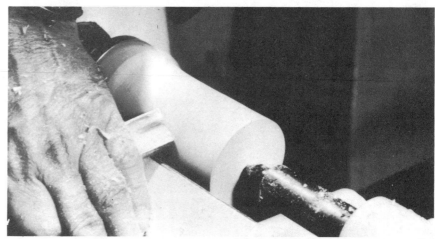

D *Marking out*

E *Marking out with parting tool*

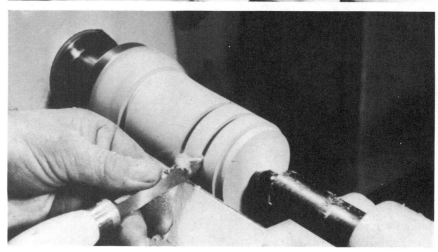

Leave a fragment of waste wood on the tailstock end and keep well away from the faceplate screws at the headstock end. The technique in box turning is to cut the lid with its inside facing the tailstock.

First of all, using the round-nose gouge, rough turn the box to shape, and remove as much of the timber as possible between the outside of the lid and the top of the box where, in fact, the knob is situated.

F *Shaping the inside of the lid*

G *Shaping the lid with the skew chisel*

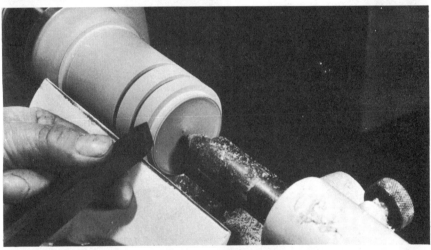

H *Shaping the lid and knob—gouging from the left*

Take a parting tool and carefully cut the rebate to the diameter of size exactly equal to the internal diameter of the box itself. Use the round-nose gouge to turn the inside surface of the lid. Here, once again, the bevel of the tool will be facing the wood, with the tool resting firmly on the tee-rest, on its side and pushed carefully from the outside to the centre close to the dead centre position. Square the edge with the long corner of the chisel.

Remove the tailstock and carefully take off the neb with the gouge so that the inside of the lid is perfectly clean and free from blemish at the centre. Clean up as necessary to leave the surface perfect. Now, part off the lid with its incomplete knob and place on one side.

Remove the dead centre from the tailstock and replace it with a tail-stock chuck. Place in the chuck a sawtooth cutter of size equal to the internal diameter of the box. With the lathe stopped and the tee-rest removed, bring up the tailstock so that the brad point of the sawtooth cutter is just touching the wood. Rotate the box by hand so that the sawtooth cutter brad point scores the centre.

Operate the clamping lever on the tailstock to fix it in this position and select the speed of the lathe most suitable to the size of sawtooth cutter in use. Switch on the lathe and advance the sawtooth cutter by operating the wheel of the tailstock.

J *Shaping the lid and knob—gouging from the right*

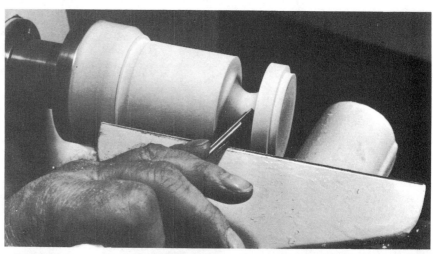

K *Parting off the lid*

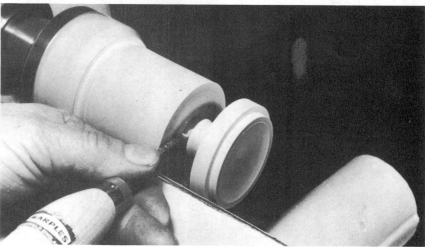

Wind the sawtooth cutter quickly into the timber at a rate of feed sufficiently fast but not fast enough to slow the lathe down. Take out the waste wood in the box body completely at one go, remove the sawtooth cutter and, if necessary, paper the inside of the box to a smooth surface. Generally, a sawtooth cutter will leave a perfectly fine surface on the inside but should the wood be 'woolly' or unusually cross-grained, it may be necessary to use glasspaper. Remove the sawtooth cutter from the tailstock and replace the dead centre. Secure the lid in place in the box body and carefully bring up the dead centre, putting a small disc of wood between the dead centre and the knob of the box. Bring the tee-rest back into position and carefully turn down the box and lid to its final outside diameter.

Carefully finish off the cutting of the knob and throughout this operation use the round-nose gouge. Remove the tailstock and very carefully, with the gouge resting on the tee-rest and its bevel facing the top of the knob, surface the knob to remove the small neb which may have been left when the work was parted off in the first place.

Remove the tee-rest and burnish the finished box with shavings.

L *Sawtooth machine cutter set up for boring*

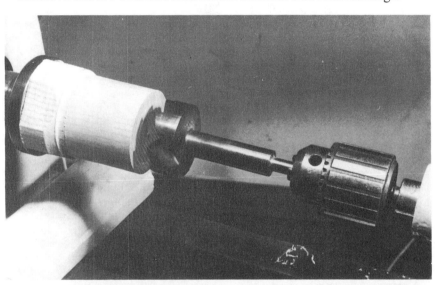

M *Boring the box body*

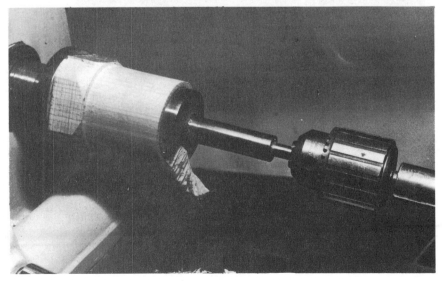

Polish the box as necessary with the lid in position. When this is completed, remove the lid, bring the tee-rest back into position and very carefully part off the box using the parting tool, widening the parting groove as the tool penetrates.

Leave sufficient timber so that a very fine parting cut can be made to leave a smooth surface on the end grain, bearing in mind that the parting tool will tend to turn over the end fibres when carrying out this type of cutting. When parting off, the tailstock can be brought up so that the dead centre protrudes into the box; this will receive the box if fully parted off in error. With the box finally parted off, the bottom can be improved by rubbing it on an abrasive board of fairly fine glasspaper. Many variations of boxes can be made in this way and, similarly, vases can be made by using the same technique, but omitting the lid procedure.

The sawtooth cutter will be found most useful for all this type of boring work, but flatbits could be substituted if their size is not greater than 1½ in. (38 mm).

N *Lid placed in position, trimming with the skew chisel from the left*

O *Trimming with the skew chisel from the right*

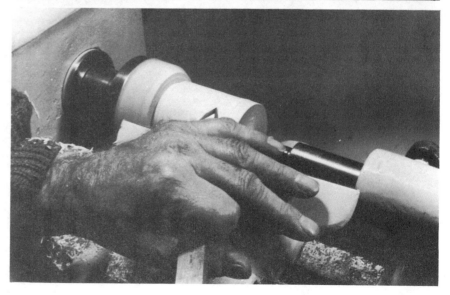

P *Using the ¼ in. gouge to finish the top of the knob*

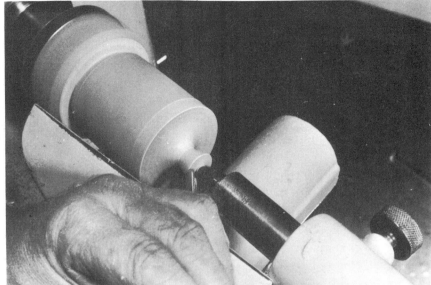

Q *Burnishing with shavings*

R *Box in ash—parting off the completed box*

Turning a shallow dish

Fig. 12.5
A *Shallow dish in Circassian walnut*

Make a sketch of the proposed design and select a clean even-coloured piece of sycamore. Sycamore is the accepted timber for domestic woodware and will give long service without staining or discolouring. The timber should be approximately ¾ in. (19 mm) thick or slightly more and is mounted on a screw chuck. Screw chuck screws tend to be rather thick in gauge and too long for this thickness of timber. The turner is advised, therefore, to use at least one disc of ⅛ in. (3 mm) thick hardboard between the dish and the screw chuck, preferably of diameter greater than that of the dish to reduce the length of screw passing into the wood. The hardboard disc will also assist rigidity during turning.

Place the screw chuck on the lathe and bring up the tee-rest. Use a shallow round-nose gouge to bring the disc down to the desired diameter.

B *Roughing down to diameter*

Stop the lathe and re-position the tee-rest across the face of the disc. Mark out the limits of the shaping with a pencil. Mark out with the parting tool. Again use the round-nose gouge to shape the outside of the dish to the suggested design. Clean off, burnish with shavings and polish as necessary.

C *Marking out—outside*

D *Marking out with the parting tool*

E *Shaping with the ½ in. spindle gouge*

F *Shaping centre recess with ¼ in. gouge*

G *Shallow dish—shaping*

H *Shaping of outside completed*

J *Polishing the outside*

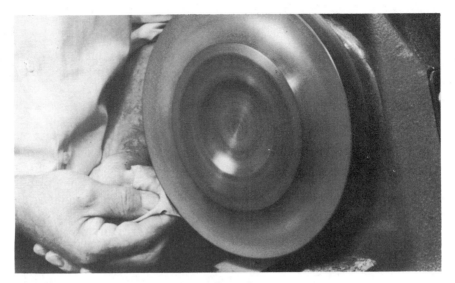

We must now prepare the chuck to receive the half-finished dish, so that the inside can be turned. Remove the screw chuck from the lathe and mount to a faceplate a block of timber of diameter greater than that of the dish by at least 1 in. (25 mm) and approximately 1½ in. (38 mm) thick. This block is to be used to make the chuck to hold the dish, so that the inside may be safely turned. Turn the 1½ in. disc down to the round and change the tee-rest to cut across the face. Mark out the size of recess necessary to hold the dish, using the parting tool. Remove the centre to indicate the depth and take out the recess using the round-nose gouge or the deep-fluted gouge, ground square across. Cut to a depth sufficient to allow the dish to be accommodated easily. The sides of the recess should be slightly tapered towards the inside in order to squeeze the dish home comfortably. Try the fitting of the dish several times while cutting the recess to ensure a good fit. Remove the tee-rest, push the dish into the recess cut in the wood chuck and be sure that it is a comfortable push fit.

K *Dish reversed and mounted in a wood chuck prepared to receive it*

Before actually placing the dish in position it may be as well to bore a hole by using the gouge or a flatbit mounted in the tailstock right through the wood chuck. This is a safety precaution made in case the dish should be so firmly fixed in the wood chuck after turning that it is difficult to remove. A dowel carefully pushed through the back can then be used to remove it, should the need arise. Bring up the tee-rest as close to the work as possible and slightly above centre height. This again is a safety precaution, since should the dish become loose with the tee-rest placed slightly above centre, it cannot actually leave the chuck and will enable the turner to stop the lathe and carefully press it back into place before continuing turning. Now use the gouge and carefully cut the dish to shape, remembering to start cutting from a small groove near the periphery of the dish, resting the gouge on its side, letting the bevel rub and traversing the tool in an arcing movement so that its centre ends exactly in the centre of the dish.

With cutting completed, burnish the dish with shavings or scrape as necessary with the lathe stopped. Polish, and carefully remove the dish.

L *½ in. gouge used to cut the dish*

M *Cutting completed—burnishing with shavings*

N *Polishing*

A very thin section should be aimed at, and here the turner must be careful to have very sharp tools and allow them to cut the wood lightly, so that no spiralling occurs on the face of the dish and a perfect surface is obtained without any pressure being applied to the dish from the tool. The wood chuck method is one which has been used down the years for holding timber, to avoid having screw holes in the finished job. In making plates and small dishes in this way, a very thin section can be obtained which would be impossible if the timber was held with screws to a faceplate or by the single screw of a screw-flange chuck. Alternatively, the timber could, of course, be held with the glue-and-paper method, but this is time-consuming. There is also great danger, if the timber has been brought to a thin section, of the wood splitting when being removed, even though the paper should, in fact, be weaker than the timber itself.

Turning a mirror frame

Prepare a design and select the timber for the job. Any of the home-grown timbers will be found suitable, but should the frame be of very narrow section a close-grained hardwood is essential.

Fig. 12.6
A *Mirror frame in sycamore*

Mount the timber on the screw chuck as before and, if using thin timber, reduce the length of the screw by adding at least one ⅛ in. (3 mm) disc of hardboard before mounting the disc itself.

Turn down the disc to round.

B *Mirror frame—disc prepared with two ⅛ in. hardboard discs*

C *Mirror frame—disc mounted and tee-rest in position*

D *Mirror frame—turning to round*

Place the tee-rest across the face of the timber and use a gouge to take a flat cut to level the face. When the surface is flat and of an even texture, use a parting tool to cut a recess to receive the mirror and cut it of sufficient depth not only to receive the mirror but also a disc of hardboard or plywood to act as a backing for the mirror.

Finish off the back of the frame and polish if necessary.

E *Mirror frame—cutting the rebate*

F *Mirror frame—rebate finished*

G *Mirror frame—shaping the back*

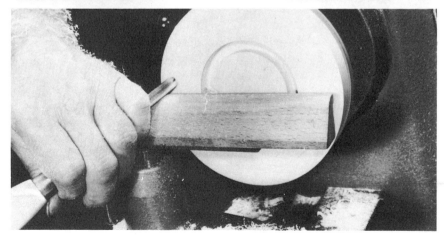

Before the lathe stops, mark the centre with a pencil, stop the lathe and use a bradawl to cut a small hole. Remove the disc from the screw chuck and reverse it, mounting it on the accurately centred hole cut with the bradawl. Use the round-nose gouge to shape up the face of the mirror frame, bringing the surface to a final finish.

H *Mirror frame—shaping with the gouge (1)*

J *Mirror frame—shaping with the gouge (2)*

K *Mirror frame—parting off*

With the parting tool, carefully cut into the internal diameter of the mirror frame but not to the point of part. Stop within ⅛ in. (3 mm) of this and remove the tee-rest. Complete the final finishing and polishing of the outside of the mirror frame. When this is completed to the turner's satisfaction, bring the tee-rest back into place and this time slightly higher than centre. Adjust the lathe to run at its lowest speed and carefully, by using the parting tool, part off the mirror frame.

If the turner listens carefully, it is possible to stop the lathe just at the point of part, with the mirror frame held by the last few fibres. However, do not worry if it should break free because it will rotate on the boss of material left on the screw chuck. Stop the lathe immediately and carefully remove the mirror frame. The tiny portion of wood which was finally cut through by the parting tool can be carefully cleaned up with a round dowel wrapped with fine glasspaper and polished as the remainder of the mirror frame. The disc for the rear, which will hold the mirror in place, can be turned on the screw chuck that was used for turning the mirror frame. The hole remaining in the centre when the disc has been cut to size need not be unsightly and, in any case, will not be seen.

Turning a pepper mill

Fig. 12.7
A *Pepper mill*

Design specification

Mill mechanisms can be obtained in various sizes and different types. The design of the outside of the mill should provide a good grip in use, and cleaning should be easy.

Finish

Use an oil finish to seal against contamination and ingress of moisture.

Timber

Use a hard-wearing timber which will remain unmarked by constant handling and association with food.

Attachment to the lathe

Use the collar chuck, since the height will vary with the mechanism selected; the longer pieces will be held more securely in this way.

Speed

Turn at 1400 r.p.m. Bore with successive sizes of sawtooth cutter, referring each size to the speed table (see page 73).

Tools

Skew chisel, 1 in. (25 mm)
Round-nose spindle gouge, ½ in. (13 mm)
Parting tool
Sawtooth cutter
Tailstock drill chuck
Collar chuck

Method

Mount between centres. Turn down timber between centres to be held in the collar chuck.

Mark out with a pencil and the parting tool, and with a ½ in. (13 mm) gouge, shape the pepper mill and lid.

B *Timber in the collar chuck*

C *Marking out*

D *Shaping with the gouge*

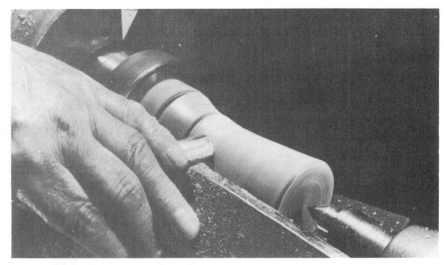

Use the long corner of the chisel to square off the body at the point of part and use the parting tool to cut a small rebate over which the top of the mill will fit. The callipers should be set to the size of the sawtooth cutter or other bit to be used in the making of the lid.

Similarly chisel the base, then shape the top with the chisel.

E *Cutting the groove which forms the rebate on which the top rotates*

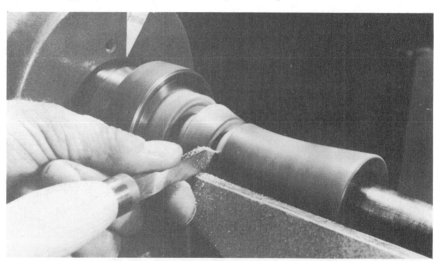

F *Trimming the sides of the rebate with the skew chisel*

Mount a sawtooth cutter of appropriate size to receive the holding bar of the mill mechanism. Change sawtooth cutter to size of mill grinding body and cut to correct depth. Change cutter to mill body size and bore to full depth of body.

Clean up, burnish with shavings and polish the body. Part off the body.

G *Trimming the base with the long corner of the skew chisel*

H *Shaping the top of the lid with the chisel*

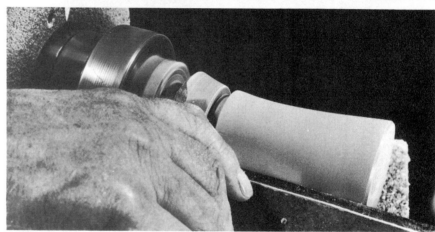

J *Boring out the body clearance hole to receive the holding bar*

K *Body boring complete*

L *Burnishing with shavings*

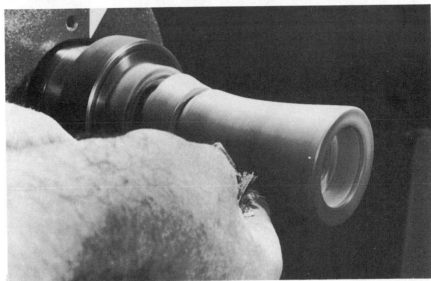

M *Polishing*

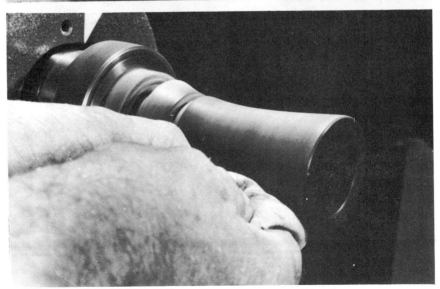

Again, set up a sawtooth cutter to cut a recess to receive the top of the mill body (that is, the rebated end). Cut a smaller recess to receive the mechanism actuating plate.

With a ⅛ in. (3 mm) cutter bore out the spindle hole.

Part off the lid after polishing—the parting tool will cut into the spindle hole to leave a clean part. Assemble the mill. Holes can also be bored using flatbits.

N *Boring the recess to receive the top of the mill body*

O *Boring the recess to receive the actuating plate*

P *Boring the spindle hole with the shell bit*

Q *Completed lid*

Alternative method for turning a pepper mill

When lathe-boring is not possible, an alternative is to pre-bore a block with holes sized to receive the mill mechanism, using any boring method available.

Prepare a piece with a Morse taper at the left-hand end exactly the same size as the taper in the headstock of the lathe to be used. Turn the right-hand end with a slight taper, so that the prepared block can be placed over it sufficiently tightly to transmit drive. Turn another piece, taper the left-hand end and leave the existing dead centre recess.

The pre-bored blank can now be placed on the lathe, using the mandrels, and turned to shape.

The top or lid of the mill will have to be turned separately.

Turning a goblet

Fig. 12.8
A *Goblet in African walnut*

Design specification

A drinking vessel having a bowl mounted on a slim stem and pedestal. From timber 8 in. (200 mm) × 4 in. (100 mm) × 4 in. (100 mm).

Finish

An acid catalyst finish; three coats, each cut back to give an eggshell finish impervious to heat or moisture.

Timber

A non-tasting timber is necessary, such as sycamore or any of the fruit timbers.

Attachment to the lathe

Screwed to a 4 in. (100 mm) faceplate with four 1¼ in. (32 mm) No. 10 screws.

Speed

Turn at 1400 r.p.m. Bore at appropriate speed for the sawtooth cutter. Part off at 600 r.p.m.

Tools

Gouges, ½ in. (13 mm) and ¼ in. (6 mm) round nose, 1 in. (25 mm) square
Parting tool
Chisel, 1 in. (25 mm)
Sawtooth cutters, 1½ in. (38 mm) and 2 in. (50 mm).

Method

Mount the block to the faceplate, screw to lathe, bring up the tailstock and tool rest.

Using the 1 in. (25 mm) square gouge, rough down to 3¾ in. (95 mm) round and plane with the chisel.

Mark out the job in pencil. Using parting tool to mark points of start.

Remove the tailstock, mount the tailstock chuck and 2 in. (50 mm) sawtooth cutter. Bore out bowl to a depth of 2 in.

B *Planing down to size*

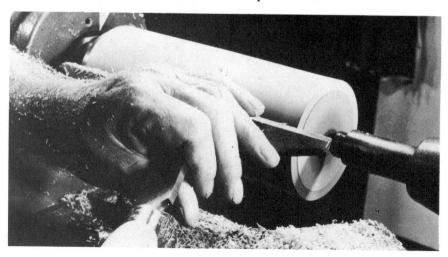

C *Marking out*

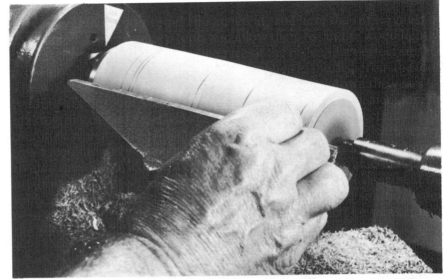

D *Marking out with the parting tool*

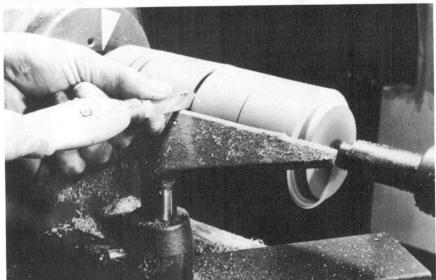

E *Boring out the waste with a saw-tooth cutter*

Substitute 1½ in. (38 mm) cutter to bore to a depth of a further 1½ in. making a total depth of 4 in. (100 mm). Cut a point of start groove.

Turn out the bowl to shape, then turn the outer shape of bowl, stem and base.

Begin to part off. Square the base edge with the long corner of the skew chisel. Burnish with shavings.

F *Cutting the point of start, before cutting inside of bowl*

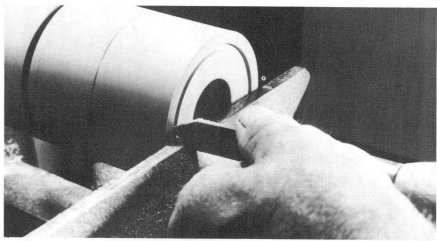

G *Using the gouge to cut the bowl—first cuts*

H *Final cuts with the ½ in. gouge*

J *Shaping the outside of the bowl*

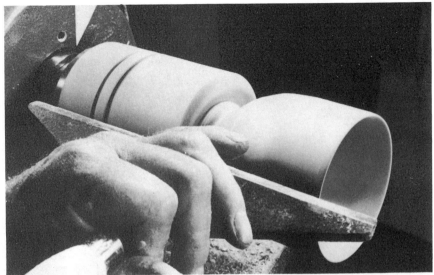

K *Shaping the base and stem*

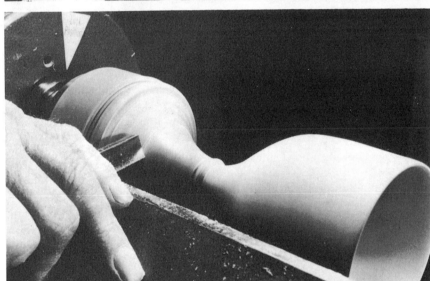

L *Turning a bead on the base with the skew chisel*

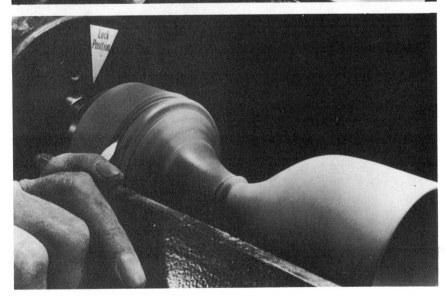

Finishing

Mix up the two-part acid catalyst polish. Apply with the lathe stationary. When dry, cut back with fine steel wool—lathe running. Apply three coats, each burnished with the lathe running, to reach a final eggshell finish.

Part off, clean up base and glue on a cork pad.

M *Preparing to part off*

N *Squaring the base with the skew chisel*

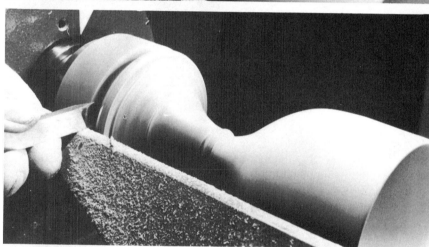

O *Burnishing the completed turning with shavings*

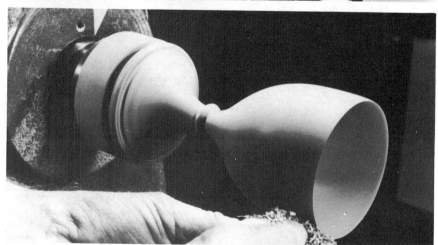

P *Polishing*

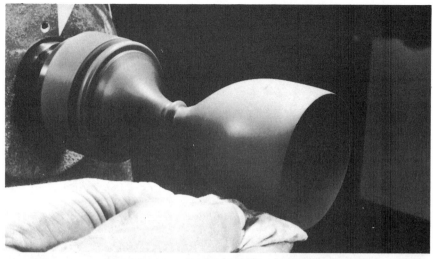

Q *The finished job ready for parting off*

Turning a small picture frame

Design specification

A frame to hold miniature photographs.

Finish

Any hard finish will be suitable; possibly seal with french polish, then polish with wax.

Timber

Small work can serve to use up those pieces of exotic timbers too small for other use.

Attachment to the lathe

A hole bored in the timber to form the recess to receive the picture will also serve to hold the timber for turning. Use either a wooden mandrel (see page 32) or the removable head mandrel (see page 33).

Speed

Turn at 1400 r.p.m.

Tools

Sawtooth cutter of size equal to the diameter of the mandrel to be used.

Round-nose spindle gouge, ¼ in. (6 mm)

Method

Bore out selected timber with sawtooth cutter to fit the metal mandrel. Assemble to the lathe, bring up the tool rest and turn down to round.

Use the gouge to shape the frame. Cut the centre out using the spindle gouge.

Bring to a finish and finally polish.

Fig. 12.9
A *Picture frames and mandrel*

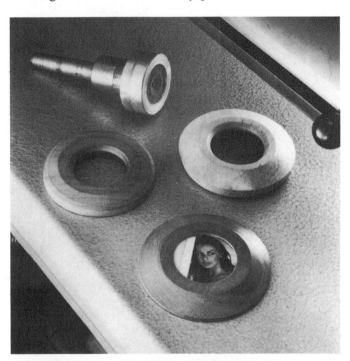

B *Turning to round*

C *Timber bored for mounting to mandrel*

D *Shaping*

E *Removing the centre*

F *Polishing*

Turning a salt dish

Design specification
   Small dish to hold table salt.

Finish
   Mazola or other cooking oil to give a non-contaminating finish, and one which will also handle well in fairly greasy conditions.

Timber
   Any close-grained hardwood will be suitable.

Attachment to the lathe
   Use the glue chuck and attach using the hot melt glue gun.

Speed
   Turn at 1400 r.p.m.

Tools
   Carry out the complete turning with ¼ in. (6 mm) spindle gouge. Mark out with the parting tool.

Fig. 12.10

A *Salt dish in Circassian walnut*

Method

Assemble timber to the glue chuck and attach to the lathe. Bring up the tool rest and turn down to round.

Shape the outside with the gouge.

Place tool rest across the face of the disc and use the parting tool to mark out the inside diameter; this groove will also act as a point of start.

B *Blank attached to the glue chuck and turned to round*

C *Turning to round*

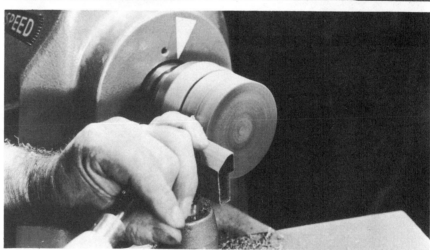

D *Shaping with small gouge*

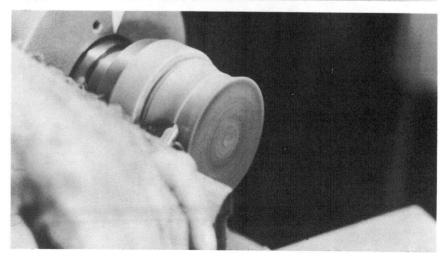

With the gouge, remove the waste, starting at the groove and running into the centre.

Shape. Make the final finishing cut. Burnish with shavings. Polish with Mazola oil.

Remove the completed dish from the glue chuck, by using a thin knife and tapping with a hammer.

E *Marking internal diameter with parting tool*

F *¼ in. gouge removing the waste*

G *Using the gouge*

H *Finishing cut taken with the gouge*

J *Burnishing with shavings*

K *Polishing*

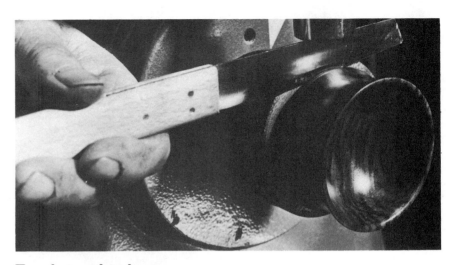

Turning a ring box

Design specification

Small box, with lid, to hold a number of rings or small pieces of jewellery.

Finish

Seal with white french polish and wax.

Timber

A well-marked colourful timber, such as yew, plum or other fruit timber, hornbeam, holly or laburnum.

Attachment to the lathe

Lid—use the glue chuck and attach using the hot melt glue gun.
Body—turn on the screw chuck.

Speed

Turn at 1400 r.p.m., bore with sawtooth cutter referring speed to size of hole (see page 73).

Tools

Round-nose gouges, ½ in. (13 mm) and ¼ in. (6 mm)
Skew chisel, 1 in. (25 mm)
Parting tool
Sawtooth cutter of appropriate size.
Tailstock drill chuck
Glue chuck or small faceplate

Method

Assemble timber for the box to the screw chuck and mount on the lathe. Bring up the tailstock dead centre and tool rest. Turn to round using the ½ in. (13 mm) gouge. Plane with 1 in. (25 mm) chisel. Shape with chisel and ¼ in. (6 mm) gouge. Remove tailstock, mount sawtooth cutter in tailstock drill chuck. Bore out the box.

Clean up as necessary.

Finishing

Seal with two coats of white french polish, burnish with shavings and/or fine steel wool.

Finally, polish with hard wax or Briwax. Remove from the screw chuck by inserting a knife.

Turning the lid

Prepare a disc and assemble to glue chuck. Cut rebate in size equal to the inside box size. Shape the lid.

Clean up, polish as for box, and remove with the knife.

Fig. 12.11
A *Laburnum ready for mounting to screw chuck to make box*

B *Boring box with Ridgway saw-tooth cutter*

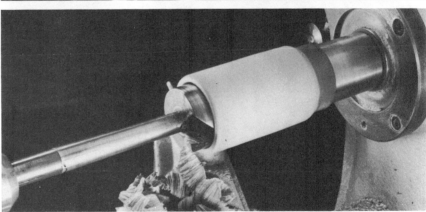

C *Turning a lid in rosewood*

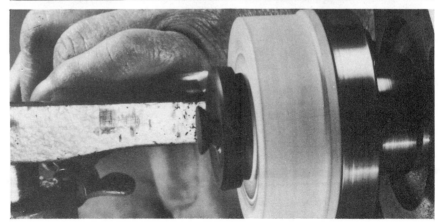

Turning a spoon

Design specification

A small spoon for a salt dish or mustard pot. The bowl can either be part-turned and carved or left in the flat.

Finish

Mazola or other cooking oil to give a non-contaminating finish.

Timber

Close-grained timber.

Attachment to the lathe

For very small spoons, mount the timber between the mandrel with the pyramidal hole and the rotating dead centre.

Speed

Turn at 1400 r.p.m.

Tools

Spindle gouge, ¼ in. (6 mm)
Skew chisel, ½ in. (13 mm)

Fig. 12.12
A *Spoon (finished)*

B1 *Sketch of blank*

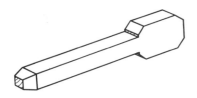

Method

Prepare a blank as shown, and mount it to the lathe.

Rough down to shape using the gouge; remember to do the heavier cutting of the bowl end first.

Shape with gouge and chisel. The turning must be cut with the tool bevels rubbing; the smallness of the timber will only permit light cutting. Scrapers cannot be used. The learner will find this project to be an excellent way to perfect his cutting techniques.

B2 *Driving mandrel with prepared blank*

C *Blank placed between mandrel and dead centre*

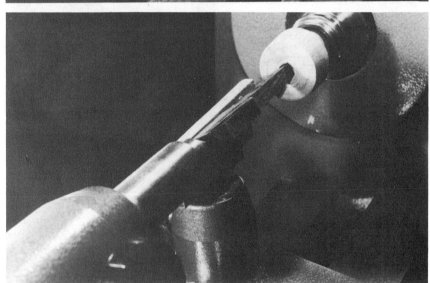

The bowl will need to be carved. To carry out the carving, lower the tool rest and slide it underneath the bowl of the spoon to support it while carving. Use a small gouge and finish with a tiny scraper and fine abrasive paper.

Finally, burnish with shavings and oil polish.

D *Roughing to size with the gouge*

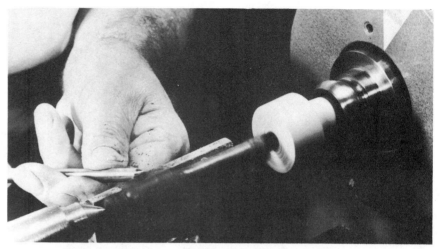

E *Planing with the chisel*

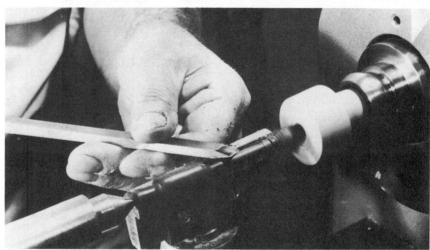

F *Shaping with the chisel*

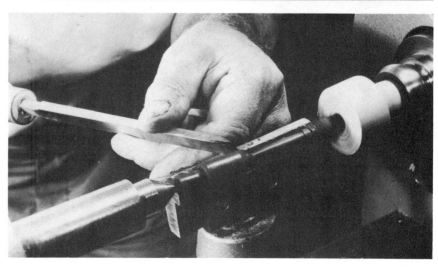

G *Shaping with the chisel*

H *Carving the bowl with a carving gouge*

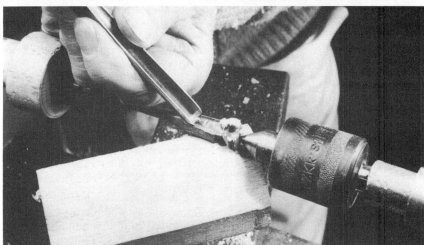

Turning serviette rings—1

Design specification

Rings to hold linen serviettes, easily cleaned. Turn at least three or four at each turning.

Fig. 12.13
A *Serviette rings in cherry*

Finish

Seal and polish with a two-part acid catalyst polish.

Timber

Any colourful close-grained hardwood can be used.

Attachment to the lathe

Turned between centres to fit and be secured in a 2 in. (50 mm) collar chuck.

Speed

Turn at 1400 r.p.m. and bore with sawtooth cutter at appropriate speed.

Tools

Chisel, 1 in. (25 mm)
Round-nose gouge, ¼ in. (6 mm)
Parting tool
Sawtooth cutter or flatbit, 1¼ in. (32 mm)

Method

Place the selected timber between centres, bring up the tailstock and tool rest. Turn down using gouge and chisel, leaving a flange at one end so that the timber can be assembled to the collar chuck.

Mount the collar chuck to the headstock, bring tailstock and tool rest into position. Mark out with pencil.

Use parting tool to cut the separating grooves between each serviette ring; cut down so that the core diameter is fractionally less than the final inside arc of the rings.

With gouge and chisel, shape each separate ring. Several different designs are suggested.

Square the ends with the long corner of the skew chisel. Burnish with shavings. Polish.

Set up a sawtooth cutter in the tailstock drill chuck of diameter equal to the inside diameter of the serviette rings.

B *Timber fitted through collar*

C *Timber with collar screwed down*

D *Collar chuck screwed on to the lathe*

E *Timber marked out*

F *Marking out with parting tool*

G *Shaping with the gouge*

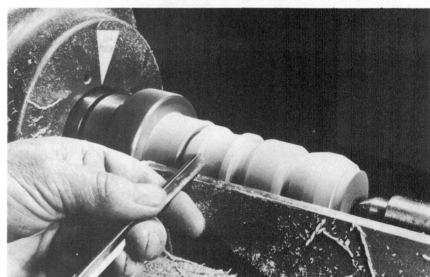

H *Shaping with the skew chisel*

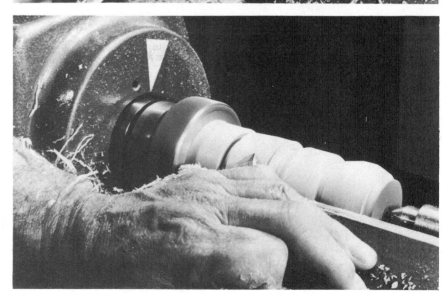

J *Squaring the ends with the skew chisel*

K *Burnishing with shavings*

L *Polishing*

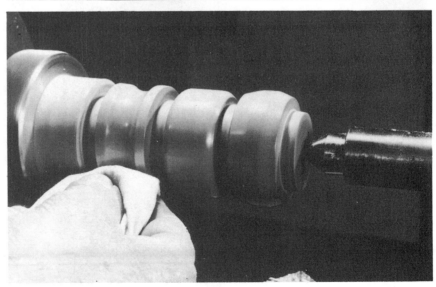

Bring up the cutter, bore out each ring.

The rings will drop over the shank of the cutter as each parting groove is reached.

Turn down the remaining stump to use as a mandrel for re-chucking each serviette ring in turn. Mount each ring, clean up each end and polish.

An alternative method for turning serviette rings is given on page 171.

M *Boring out with the sawtooth cutter—scoring the centre*

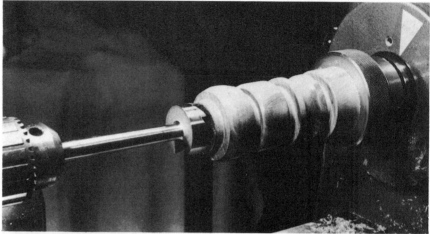

N *Boring out with the sawtooth cutter*

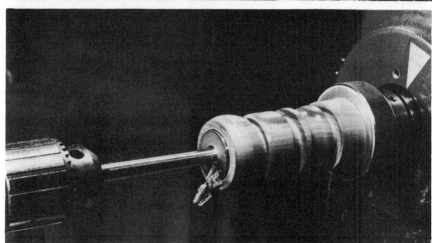

O *First ring bored and parted off*

P *Second ring bored and parted off*

Q *Third ring bored and parted off*

R *Stump used as mandrel to remount each ring for end finishing*

S *Mounted on mandrel—polishing*

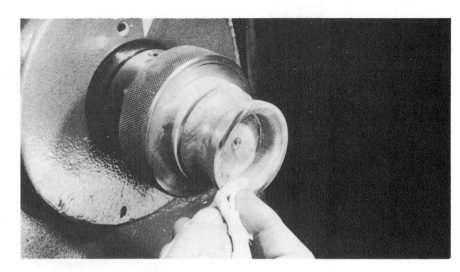

Turning an egg-cup

Prepare blanks for mounting to the screw chuck.

Mount to the lathe, turn down to round and mark out sizes with a parting tool.

Use a boring bit to remove some of the waste, then shape; alternatively, use a small gouge to cut the bowl entirely.

Fig. 12.14
A *Egg-cup (finished)*

B *Egg-cup turning to round*

A small curved scraper can also be used to shape the bowl, working from the inside outwards. This will be cutting with the grain and a finely sharpened scraper will produce shavings.

It is always advisable to carry out the bowl-cutting operation first in this particular work.

Now shape the outside of the egg-cup, including the base, taking care not to over-decorate so as to make the article difficult to keep clean.

Polish and remove from the chuck.

C *Turning the cup using ¼ in. gouge*

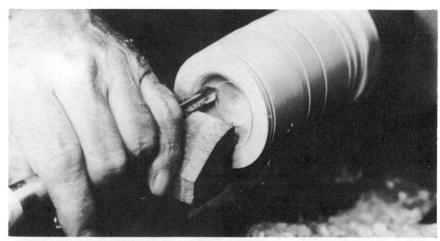

D *Marking out with parting tool*

E *Turning the tray with the gouge*

Finishing the base

Prepare an egg-shaped mandrel with Morse taper to suit your particular lathe. Alternatively, turn on a screw centre—the only disadvantage with this method is that if the half-egg is to be used repeatedly, it is doubtful whether accurate centring will be possible each time, whereas a Morse taper chuck can be used for many years.

Insert this in the headstock, place the egg-cup in position and bring up the tailstock to secure. Use the small tailstock mandrel from the pepper mill assembly between the base of the cup and the dead centre.

Trim off the waste and slightly incurve the base.

The small centre neb on the base can be removed with a small chisel after removal from the lathe.

F *Egg-cup mandrel*

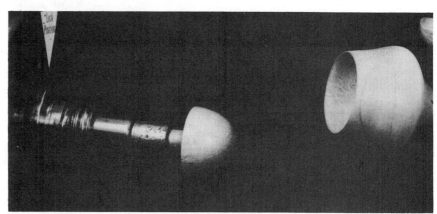

G *Egg-cup mounted between mandrel and tailstock*

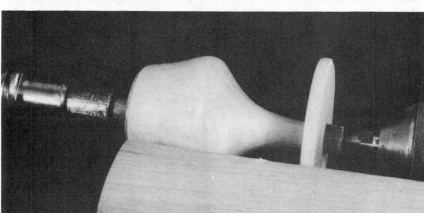

H *Egg-cup—cleaning up the underside of the base*

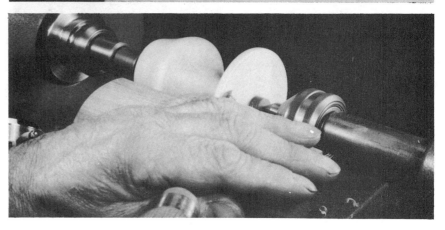

Turning wheels

Turning a number of wheels to exact size and shape can present a problem, particularly to the youngster at school or the home craftsman.

Prepare two discs, A and B, 1 in. (25 mm) thick by 3 in. (75 mm) in diameter. Bore a ¼ in. (6 mm) hole in the centre of each, halfway through. Prepare the opposite side of disc A to receive the lathe rotating centre and the opposite side of disc B to receive the driving fork. Finally, a piece of ¼ in. (6 mm) dowel rod C will be cut to a length fractionally less than the total thickness of the wheel discs plus the depth of the two holes.

To turn the wheels, cut the required number of blanks, bore a ¼ in. (6 mm) hole in the centre of each. Calculate the length of dowel required by using the following formula: number of wheels times thickness of wheels plus half-thickness of the prepared end discs minus ⅛ in. (3 mm). The ⅛ in. allowance will permit the blanks to be squeezed tightly together, since an over-long dowel may prevent this. Place the wheel blanks on the dowel rod, add both end discs and put the complete assembly in the lathe. Tighten up securely using the tailstock.

Turn the wheels down to size; they can have shaped rims, cutting as for beading. Finish as necessary and remove from the lathe.

Further shaping of each face can be carried out by attaching each wheel, using a round-headed screw and washer to secure it to a block attached to a faceplate. Alternatively, each wheel can be inserted into one of the wood chucks previously described.

Fig. 12.15
A *Preparation of discs*

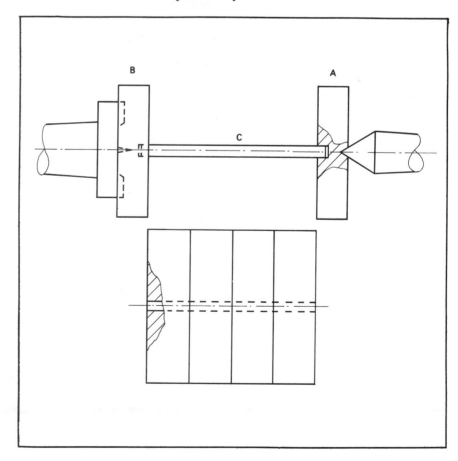

B *Blanks mounted between prepared discs*

C *Turning down to diameter*

D *Shaping with the chisel*

E *Finished wheels*

Turning a hand mirror

Fig. 12.16
A *Front-mounted hand mirror*

Select a suitable disc of close-grained hardwood. Plane one side flat and attach the disc by this face to the glue chuck. Turn down to size using a ¼ in. or ⅜ in. (6 or 9.5 mm) gouge; cut a recess to receive the mirror. A slightly larger recess is suggested than the diameter of the mirror. Complete and polish.

B *Disc assembled on the screw chuck*

C *Turning to size*

D *Cutting the mirror recess—marking diameter with parting tool*

E *Cutting mirror recess with the gouge*

F *Outside shaping*

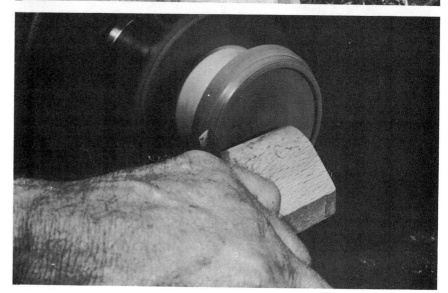

G *Hand mirror—polishing*

Plane a suitable piece of timber for the handle and turn down to size with a gouge. Plane with the chisel and use the chisel and gouge to shape the handle. Cut a small tenon to insert into the frame. Polish and remove from the lathe.

Bore a hole in the frame to receive the tenon of the handle. Glue up and polish final coat.

H *Handle blank: assemble using mandrel with square hole*

I *Handle: roughing down*

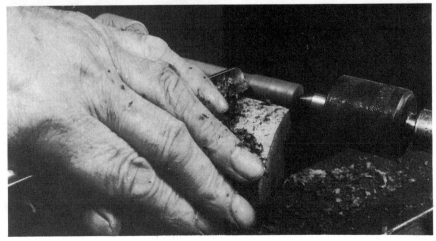

J *Handle: shaping*

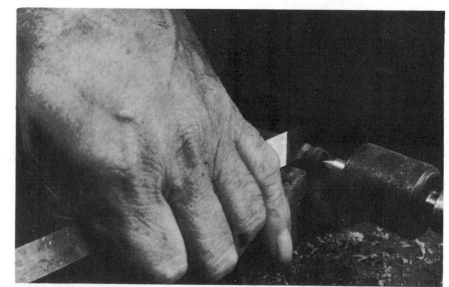

K *Handle: using the chisel*

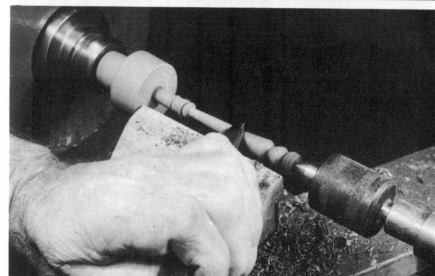

L *Handle: polishing*

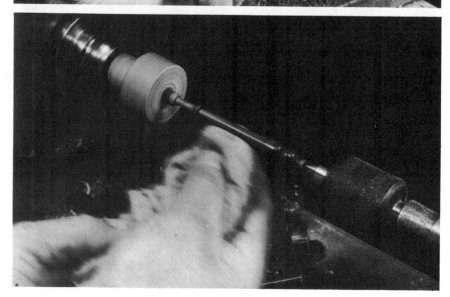

Turning a key tag

Prepare a suitable length of close long-grained hardwood to mount between centres.

Turn to shape using a ¼ in. (6 mm) gouge and a ½ in. (13 mm) chisel. Polish.

Part off and bore a small hole to receive key ring.

Fig. 12.17
A *Key tag in lignum vitae*

B *Key tag—chiselling on lathe*

Turning a bottle stopper

Turn the stopper from a close-grained hardwood, which can be sealed effectively against the ingress of moisture.

Mount between centres, use a small gouge and chisel to turn to shape.

Seal, polish and part off.

B *Turning between centres—*
squaring the shoulder

Fig. 12.18
A *Bottle stopper*

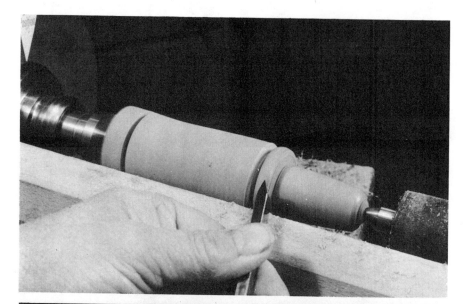

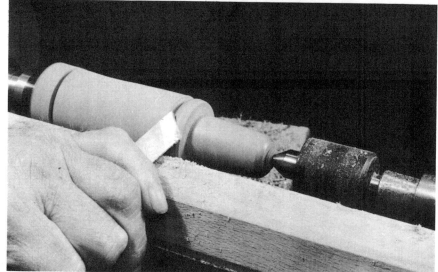

C *Rounding over (beading)*

D *Chiselling the taper*

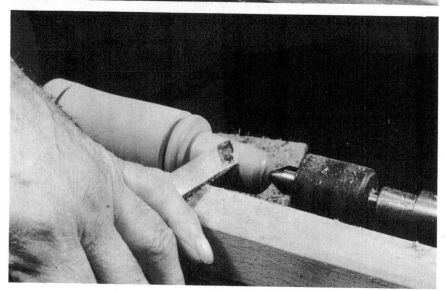

E Shaping the top

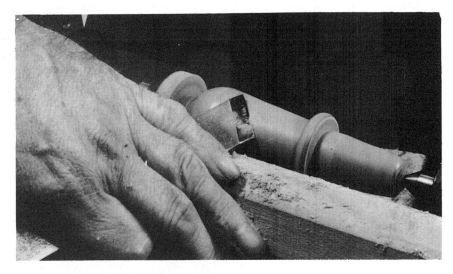

Turning a wooden egg

Choose a piece of wood with marked grain. Place between centres and turn down to round. Mark out the turned cylinder and use gouge and chisel to turn to shape. Burnish with shavings.

Finish, polish and part off.

Fig. 12.19
A *Wooden egg in yew*

B *Roughing with the deep gouge*

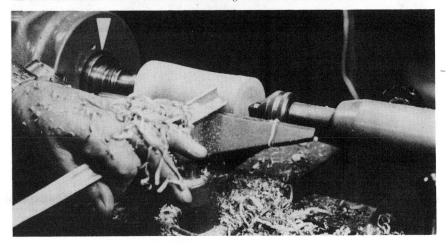

C *Shaping with the chisel*

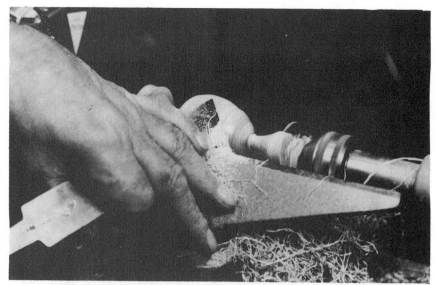

D *Burnishing with shavings*

E *Parting off*

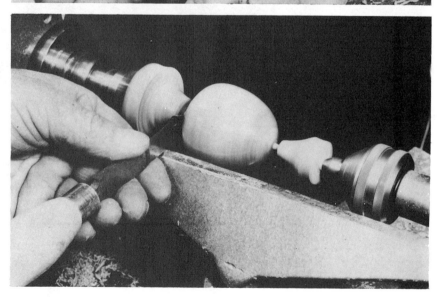

Turning a pendant mirror

This is another mini-turning exercise.

Place a disc, preferably of one of the more exotic timbers, on the glue chuck. Turn down to size, shape, cut a recess to receive the mirror. Polish and remove from the chuck.

Turn between centres the small components, leaving a tenon for assembly to the mirror frame. Polish and part off.

Glue up the pendant and glue the mirror in place using an epoxy resin glue.

The pendant can be suspended with a leather thong.

Fig. 12.20
Pendant mirror

Turning serviette rings—2

An alternative method of making serviette rings is first of all to prepare a mandrel on which the pre-bored material will be mounted for turning.

A long and straight-grained piece of hardwood should be turned between centres and planed with a skew chisel to a diameter equal to the inner diameter of the serviette ring. Turn the mandrel with a slight taper from left to right.

Fig. 12.21
A *Serviette ring (alternative method)*

Push one of the bored blocks over the mandrel. Use gouge and chisel to shape and size the ring.

To shape the inside of the ring, make a small wood chuck. This can be mounted on a screw chuck and bored out with a cutting tool or a saw-tooth cutter. Leave the inside of the hole rough to give added grip.

Push each serviette ring in turn into the chuck and cut the inside to shape. Polish before removing.

B *Preparing a mandrel*

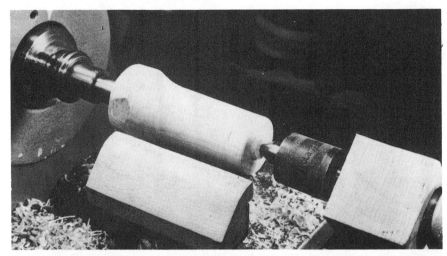

C *Pre-bored material mounted on mandrel*

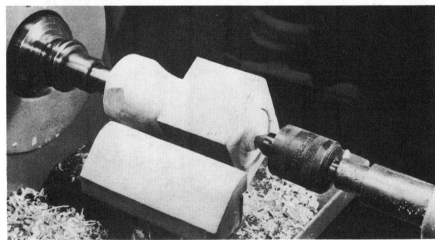

D *Turning the ring*

13 Accessories for the Woodturner

An awareness of the accessories available to the woodturner can make for improved designs and give greater satisfaction, whether the turner is working for his own pleasure or for profit.

Glassware

Condiment liners

Up to 2 in. (50 mm) diameter, these liners are available in plain or blue glass. Ideal for salt and mustard pots. Can also be used for candle inserts.

Egg-timer glasses

These glasses are pear shaped, in several colours, and are usually marked up in 3-, 4-, and 5-minute graduations.

Glass inserts

Up to 6 in. (150 mm) diameter, and available in both plain and blue glass. These inserts can also be in various depths. Useful for ashtrays, butter dishes, cheese dishes and sundry other foods. They can be used as inserts and also fitted with lids.

Hors-d'oeuvre dish inserts

These inserts are available in sets of six, making up a complete circular dish up to 12 in. (300 mm) in diameter. They are usually in clear decorated glass or in blue glass.

Hour-glasses

There is available a twin-bulb style, of 1-hour or ¼-hour duration, 8 in. (200 mm) high × 3 in. (75 mm) diameter, or 5 in. (125 mm) × 2 in. (50 mm). A 5-minute type is also available. These hour-glasses are made in several colours.

Ceramic tiles

Usually 6 in. (150 mm) in diameter in a wide variety of designs, these tiles are ideal for inserts in cheese dishes, teapots and coffee pot stands, ashtrays, etc. Also for mounting in picture frames.

Metal instrument components

Thermometers

Circular thermometers are available in various diameters up to 2¾ in. (70 mm) and finishes. Usually inserted.

Aneroid barometer movements

Various types, fully adjustable and temperature compensated, in several sizes, are available. Good ones are quite expensive.

Pepper mill mechanisms

There are two types of mechanism—with and without handles. Lengths are 4 in. (100 mm), 6 in (150 mm), 8 in. (200 mm) and 10 in. (250 mm).

Ship's-wheel nutcracker set in brass

These items are threaded for fixing to the nut bowl.

Hardware nut bowl set

This set comprises anvil and mallet fittings in brass.

Nutcracker set

This set consists of six picks and a spring-action nutcracker.

Table-lighter inserts

These inserts are available in many varieties of metals and types.

Clock movements

Both battery and mains types are available, in various sizes.

Revolving-top ashtrays

There are varying qualities and sizes, usually with easily removable second tray for ash disposal.

Lazy Susan bearings

These are revolving ball bearing cases for turntables, trays, cake-stands, etc., in 3 in. (75 mm), 4 in. (100 mm) and 6 in. (150 mm) sizes.

Blades for domestic use
Bread-knife blades
Cheese-knife blades
Salad servers
Steak knives and forks
Barman's knife—double-ended
Crown cork bottle opener
Corkscrew fitting
Letter opener blades

Condiment sets

These have plastic or rubber closures.

Candlestick eyelets

A number of styles are available.

Lamp stands

These items have brass nipples, one end coarse-threaded for wood, the other end a standard bulb-holder thread. The switched bulb-holders are available in plastic or metal.

Picture frame hangers

There are the brass screw-in, split-ring type and brass plates for hanging barometers, etc.

14 Work by Contemporary Woodturners

Fig. 14.1
*Chair in western red cedar, 86 cm
high. Made in 1974 by Stephen
Hogbin, Ontario*

Fig. 14.2
Walnut item, 20 cm dia. Made in 1974 by Stephen Hogbin, Ontario

Fig. 14.3
Lidded container in she oak, 17 cm high. Made in 1975 by Stephen Hogbin, Ontario. Dish in she oak, 25 cm long × 9 cm wide × 4 cm high. Made in 1975 by Stephen Hogbin, Ontario

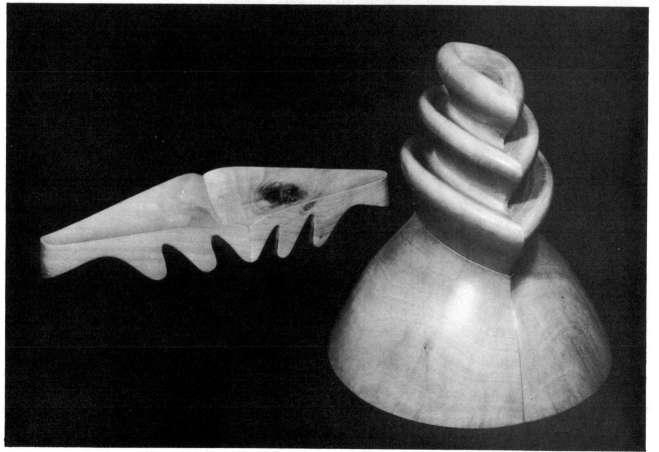

Fig. 14.4
Bowl in sassafras, 18 cm dia. × 14 cm wide. Made in 1975 by Stephen Hogbin, Ontario

Fig. 14.5
Biscuit and butter dish. Made by John Sainsbury

Fig. 14.6
*Oak fruit bowl. Made by Arthur F.
Allen*

Fig. 14.7
*Nut dish with shell waste. Made by
John Sainsbury*

Fig. 14.8
Fruit tray in Circassian walnut. Made by John Sainsbury

Fig. 14.9
Tray in yew—offset turning. Made by John Sainsbury

Fig. 14.10
Bowl in mahogany and sycamore—
laminated 55 pieces. Made by
Arthur F. Allen

Fig. 14.11
Fruit bowl in teak. Made by John
Sainsbury

Fig. 14.12
Left to right: muninga from Africa,
5 in. × 8 in; putumuju from Brazil,
3 in × 6 in.; ebony from Nigeria,
3½ in. × 6½ in. All made in 1977 by
Bob Stocksdale, California

Fig. 14.13
Drinking mugs—turned and bored on
lathe using Ridgway sawtooth cutters
and Marples turning tools

15 Glossary

ABRASIVE STICK. A rubberized abrasive for fine sharpening.

ARBOR. Usually machined to agreed sizes of Morse taper (see Morse taper) to fit the hollow mandrel of the lathe headstock or tailstock.

ARKANSAS. A natural stone quarried in Arkansas, USA: the finest natural sharpening stone available (see Black Arkansas).

ARRIS. The sharp corner on a piece of woodwork.

BACK STEADY/STAY. Used to support slender work on the lathe.

BED. Main section of the lathe, usually cast and accurately machined, on which other parts of the lathe are located.

BLACK ARKANSAS. The finest of the Arkansas stones, used for putting on the final edge.

BODGER. A turner usually working on a pole lathe, mainly turning chair legs.

CALLIPERS. Tools for measuring round stock. There are three types: *combination callipers* for inside and outside measuring, *inside callipers* for measuring internal diameters, and *outside callipers* for measuring external diameters.

CARBORUNDUM. A type of manufactured sharpening stone.

CARNAUBA. A hard wax used with beeswax or applied on its own directly to the wood.

CENTRE
   Back or dead centre. A support for the timber which is located in the tailstock—it does not rotate.
   Cup centre. A tailstock-mounted centre with finely turned centre surrounded by a rim or cup which acts as a further support for the timber and on which the timber runs.
   Driving or fork centre. One which fits in the headstock mandrel and drives the work between centres.
   Running centre. A tailstock-mounted centre which runs on ball bearings.
   Screw centre. One mounted in the headstock for holding timber.

CENTRE PUNCH. A punch used to indent the tailstock end of the timber before mounting it in the lathe.

CHISEL. A square-ended or skew tool for planing timber; also used for beading.
   Scraping chisel. A chisel available in a number of end shapes. It has a short bevel and is used to scrape timber into shape rather than cut it. Mainly used for finishing rough turned work.
   Skew chisel. A chisel with an angled cutting edge, usually ground on both sides for planing on the lathe.

CHUCK
   Coil chuck. A patented chuck using the collar chuck principle but allowing work of any size to be inserted from the front. The work is held by a coiled spring which locates in a groove on the workpiece.

Collar chuck. A special chuck with a screwed collar device to hold timber to a screwed backplate.

Collet chuck. One with a number of collets for holding small round work.

Cup chuck. One usually made in metal, with an accurate recess for holding work to be turned.

Expanding collet chuck. A unique device, using an expanding collet which locates in a recess cut in the timber.

Flange chuck or screw chuck. A metal chuck which screws to the headstock with a single screw on which the timber is mounted.

Simple chuck. A recess in a piece of wood mounted on the lathe to receive work being turned.

Split chuck. A wood chuck with cut splits and a tightening ring.

CHUCKING. Mounting the work on the lathe.

CONE PULLEY. A pulley which is usually four-stepped to give alternative speeds for the lathe.

DISTANCE BETWEEN CENTRES. The maximum length of timber which can be mounted between headstock and tailstock centres.

FACEPLATE. A plate which screws to the headstock mandrel and to which timber is attached. Can either be mounted on the left or right of the headstock. The plate can vary in size between 3 in. (75 mm) and 14 in. (355 mm).

FERRULE. A cylindrical piece of metal, either brass or steel, mounted on the blade end of the tool handle to prevent the tang of the tool splitting the handle.

FORSTNER BIT. A bit which runs on its periphery, designed for cutting shallow holes in wood.

GAP BED. A lathe bed having a gap lower than the bed itself to accommodate larger work.

GAUGE. An instrument, usually made of wood, used to check the diameter of turned work.

GOUGE. Cutting tool having a curved section, which can be shallow or deep.

HARD ARKANSAS. A special grade of Arkansas oilstone.

HEADSTOCK. That part of the lathe which houses the driven mandrel.

INDIA. A manufactured type of sharpening stone available in many shapes and sizes.

LAMINATIONS. The building up of timber in layers for woodturning.

LIP AND SPUR DRILL. A drill having a brad point for location, designed for boring wood.

MANDREL. The spindle in the headstock or tailstock which is hollowed to receive various components.

MANDREL NOSE. The screwed end of the headstock mandrel to which faceplates and other accessories are screwed.

MORSE TAPER. A standard range of taper sizes used for lathe accessories.

PARAFFIN WAX. A wax used in the melted state to seal the ends of recently cut timber or a disc cut out of the plank.

PARTING OFF. Cutting off finished work on the lathe.

PARTING TOOL. A slender chisel-like tool used to part off finished work or for marking out on the lathe.

POINT OF START. Small groove cut with the parting tool.

POLE LATHE. An ancient lathe consisting of a rope and a springy pole to provide rotation of the lathe.

ROUGHING. Bring work to the round quickly using a gouge.

R.P.M. (revolutions per minute). The speed at which the lathe spindle revolves.

RUBBERIZED SHARPENING STICKS. Aluminium oxide bonded in oil-resistant rubber—a perfect sharpening tool.

SAWTOOTH CUTTER. A machine tool cutter for large or small deep-hole boring on the lathe or drill.

SIZING TOOL. A tool used in conjunction with a parting tool for sizing work between centres.

SLIP. An oilstone shaped to use in the hollow gouges.

SPINDLE. An alternative name for the mandrel (see Mandrel).

SPINDLE TURNING. All turning work mounted between centres.

SPLIT TURNING. A turning cut through the centre.

STEADY. A component constituted in wood or metal, mounted on the bed of the lathe to the rear of the work to support slender timber when turning.

SWING. The largest diameter which can be turned on the headstock without fouling the lathe bed.

TAILSTOCK. Support for the timber at the opposite end to the headstock. Can be fixed at any point along the bed; its mandrel is adjustable and lockable.

TEE-REST. An alternative name for a tool rest (see Tool rest).

TEMPLATE. A shaped piece of metal, wood or card used to check repetition work.

TOOL REST. Tee-shaped rest for supporting the hand-held woodturning tools—also referred to as a tee-rest.

WASHITA. The fastest sharpening stone in the Arkansas range of stones.

WAX POLISH. A polish of beeswax softened in turpentine and used as a burnishing agent for turned work.

WIRE EDGE. The edge thrown up on the back or flat side of the tool when sharpening.

Index